Vegan
HOLIDAY COOKING

60 Meatless, Dairy-Free Recipes Full of Festive Flavors

KIRSTEN KAMINSKI
Creator of The Tasty K

PAGE STREET
PUBLISHING CO.

PAGE STREET
PUBLISHING CO.

First published in 2019 by
Page Street Publishing Co.
27 Congress Street, Suite 105
Salem, MA 01970
www.pagestreetpublishing.com

Distributed by Macmillan, sales in Canada by The Canadian Manda Group.

23 22 21 20 19   1 2 3 4 5

ISBN-13: 978-1-62414-906-1
ISBN-10: 1-62414-906-5

Library of Congress Control Number: 2019939666

Cover and book design by Rosie Stewart for Page Street Publishing Co.
Photography by Kirsten Kaminski
Author photos by Ana Fluieras

Printed and bound in the United States

TO EVERYONE OUT THERE, VEGAN AND NONVEGAN ALIKE, WHO IS TRYING. NO MATTER HOW BIG OR SMALL THE EFFORT, YOU ARE AMAZING!

FOR EVERYONE OUT THERE STRUGGLING WITH THEIR JOURNEY, I FEEL YOU. DON'T JUDGE TOO HARSHLY— WE ALL GET THERE EVENTUALLY.

SPREAD LOVE, APPRECIATE THE SMALL THINGS AND BE KIND TO YOURSELF AND EVERYONE AROUND YOU!

Contents

Introduction

Holidays are my favorite times of the year! They're times for celebration and happiness, when I can forget my busy everyday life for a moment, gather with loved ones and indulge in my favorite food. Some of my dearest memories from growing up are connected to the festive seasons, and food has always played such a major role in these events—from devouring my mom's heavenly cinnamon ice cream or hearty soups, to baking and frosting hundreds of cookies before Christmas, to having a big Easter brunch table filled with hot cross buns and sweet pastries.

HOLIDAY EXTRAVAGANZA

When I went vegan, one of my biggest hopes was to keep festive traditions alive by replacing animal-based dishes with mouthwatering vegan alternatives that everyone at the table would enjoy. Because I'm the only vegan in my family, it has always been a balancing act between sticking to long-kept traditions and cooking up a holiday feast that everyone—including me—can be a part of. Over the past three years, however, I have slowly but surely transformed most of my family's favorites into vegan-friendly versions. For example, last year's holiday table boasted a centerpiece of Mushroom Wellington with Gravy (page 13), sides ranging from Spiced-Apple Red Cabbage (page 27) to a Cheesy Leek-Potato Soup (page 144), delectable desserts—including a Decadent Vegan Tiramisu (page 38)—and merely one nonvegan addition. And the best part? Everyone, including the meat-loving family members, were enjoying the meal to the fullest and even asking for seconds!

Making plant-based food more accessible to the world and showing how uncomplicated, tasty and enjoyable vegan dishes can be has always been my goal. After three amazing years of creating recipes and sharing them with millions of viewers on my blog and Facebook video page, I couldn't be more excited about dedicating an entire book to my favorite holidays and the amazing foods and memories surrounding them. In this cookbook, you'll find many pieces of my childhood and most-cherished holiday experiences, arranged by holiday to help you create an extravagant vegan feast and to show the world how colorful, decadent and flavorful the vegan kitchen can be! Instead of trying to imitate meat roasts, I prefer to focus on the goodness and exciting flavors that veggies bring to the table, keeping the recipes more natural and wholesome.

ANYTIME MEALS

Even though this book is all about holiday flavors, the great thing is that the vast majority of the dishes are not limited to special occasions. You can whip them up year-round and call them lunch or dinner. While some may be a bit more connected to certain holidays, most of the dishes in this book can be served on regular weekdays or for weekend brunches!

When it comes down to it, you can treat this book as one of your go-to cookbooks. Whip up some Vegan Egg Salad (page 117) for an easy lunch, make a decadent Chocolate Yule Log (page 35) just because you can, dig into those Dijon Scalloped Potatoes (page 114) at your friend's birthday party and impress your family with a hearty Mac 'n' Cheese Bake (page 76) that will leave them wanting more!

If you have been following my journey and recipes for a while already, you might notice that the dishes in this book are a bit more on the indulgent side and include things such as oil, vegan butter and sugar. There are two main reasons for that. First, I think that if there is a time of year when we should simply enjoy our meals without worrying about their nutritional contents, it's during the holidays. Second, holidays are a few of the rare occasions when families and friends gather around the same table and feast together. I'm assuming that most families are not purely vegan or vegetarian and hence might have different tastes that are less accustomed to plant-based foods. I want the dishes and flavors in this book to be enjoyable for everyone, whether they are vegan or not, so that hopefully they'll become family favorites attached to wonderful holiday memories!

Because I want this book to be as inclusive as possible and know that many people are struggling with finding good gluten-free options, I've put extra effort into making sure that most dishes are either completely gluten free or easily adjustable. Two-thirds of the recipes in this book are gluten free by default, and you'll find notes in the remaining recipes explaining my favorite substitutions.

I couldn't be prouder of the recipes in this book, and there is no greater satisfaction for me than seeing you make and enjoy them together with your loved ones. I hope this book can become your new go-to vegan meal guide and inspire you to add more plant-based deliciousness to your life!

Happy holidays,

Kirsten Kaminsk

Fantastic No-Meat
CHRISTMAS FEASTS

Christmas is my favorite holiday—I'm an absolute sucker for the warm spices, cookies, decked halls and everything Santa! In this chapter, you'll find some amazing centerpieces to wow your guests as well as classic side dishes to go along with them.

As for the desserts, here is where this chapter truly shines. No Christmas is complete without them, and I've included some of my favorite cookie recipes as well as fancy-schmancy, super rich and decadent recipes to satisfy your sweet tooth.

Before you dive into this chapter, remember: You can use pretty much any of the recipes in Classic Thanksgiving Eats (page 65) for your Christmas menu!

MUSHROOM WELLINGTON WITH GRAVY

A juicy and flavorful mushroom, walnut and lentil mixture takes center stage in this beautiful twist on the classic Wellington. It is the perfect combination of hearty filling and crunchy crust, making this an ideal main dish for Christmas or other holiday celebrations!

YIELD: 10 servings

FILLING

2 tbsp (30 ml) olive oil

1 medium onion, diced

8 portobello mushrooms, cleaned and finely chopped

1 tbsp (3 g) fresh thyme leaves

3 cloves garlic, minced

5 tbsp (75 ml) soy sauce, divided

3 tbsp (45 ml) red wine, divided

1 (14-oz [400-g]) can lentils, drained and rinsed

½ cup (60 g) walnuts, roughly chopped

½ cup (60 g) breadcrumbs

1 tbsp (15 ml) date syrup or pure maple syrup

1 tsp Dijon mustard

½ tsp ground cinnamon

¼ tsp black pepper

¼ tsp salt

CRUST

1 sheet frozen vegan puff pastry

1 tsp almond or soy milk

Preheat the oven to 350°F (175°C). Line a medium baking sheet with parchment paper.

To make the filling, heat the oil in a large nonstick saucepan over medium heat. Add the onion and cook for 5 minutes, until it is golden brown, stirring occasionally. Add the mushrooms, thyme, garlic, 2 tablespoons (30 ml) of the soy sauce and 2 tablespoons (30 ml) of the wine. Sauté until most of the mushrooms' liquid has released and evaporated, about 10 minutes.

To make the crust, while the mushroom mixture is cooking, place the puff pastry on the prepared baking sheet and let the pastry thaw at room temperature until it unfolds easily.

In the meantime, place the lentils in a medium bowl. Use a fork to mash the lentils, leaving a few chunks here and there. Add the cooked mushroom mixture, remaining 3 tablespoons (45 ml) of soy sauce, remaining 1 tablespoon (15 ml) of wine, walnuts, breadcrumbs, syrup, mustard, cinnamon, black pepper and salt. Use a fork to mash everything together until the mixture is thick and sticky. (I like to leave some chunks for texture.)

Place the mixture in the middle of the puff pastry and, using your hands, form the mixture into a log shape, making sure to leave a 1-inch (2.5-cm) border at the ends of the pastry.

Very carefully fold the pastry ends over the mushroom mixture, then fold over the lengthwise edges so that you form a log. Use a fork to gently seal the edges and roll the log over until the pastry seam is facing downward.

With a knife, gently score the top of the Wellington diagonally, making sure not to cut too deep. Use a brush to lightly coat the top of the pastry with the almond or soy milk. Bake the Wellington for 30 minutes, until the crust is golden brown and flaky.

(continued)

GRAVY

2 tbsp (28 g) vegan butter or 2 tbsp (30 ml) olive oil

1 medium onion, diced

1 clove garlic, minced

⅓ cup (40 g) all-purpose flour

3 cups (720 ml) vegetable broth

⅓ cup (80 ml) soy milk

2 tbsp (30 ml) dark soy sauce

Salt, to taste

Black pepper, to taste

While the Wellington is baking, prepare the gravy. Heat the butter in a large saucepan over medium heat. Add the onion and sauté for 3 minutes, until it is golden brown, then add the garlic and sauté for 1 minute. Add the flour and stir until the onion is evenly coated. Add the broth, soy milk, soy sauce, salt and black pepper, stirring continuously. Reduce the heat to low and cook for 5 to 7 minutes, whisking until all the lumps have disappeared and the gravy is thick. (If needed, use more flour for an even thicker gravy or more broth for a thinner gravy.)

Once the Wellington is done, let it cool slightly before cutting it into thick slices. Serve the Wellington with the gravy.

QUICK TIP: To make the Wellington even more impressive, use festive cookie cutters to cut out additional shapes of puff pastry and place them on top of the pastry log before baking.

ROOT VEGETABLE TART WITH CANDIED NUTS

This beautiful root vegetable tart is the perfect combination of sweet and savory and a showstopper for your Christmas brunch or dinner! I love the colors and variety of textures: flaky puff pastry, melted cashew mozzarella, chunky root vegetables and crunchy candied nuts.

YIELD: 8 servings

THYME CASHEW MOZZARELLA

½ cup (75 g) raw cashews

1¼ cups (300 ml) water

2 tbsp (10 g) nutritional yeast

3 tbsp (24 g) tapioca flour

2 cloves garlic

½ tsp salt

¼ tsp black pepper

1 tbsp (3 g) fresh thyme leaves, plus more as needed

ROOT VEGETABLE TART

1 small sweet potato, peeled

1 medium carrot, peeled

1 medium parsnip, peeled

2 small beets, peeled

1 sheet frozen vegan puff pastry

To begin preparing the thyme cashew mozzarella, place the cashews in a small bowl and cover them with water. Soak the cashews for 6 to 8 hours (or overnight), then drain them and place them in a high-speed blender.

To make the root vegetable tart, bring 2 medium pots of water to a boil over high heat. Place the sweet potato, carrot and parsnip in one pot and the beets in the other. (If you don't mind the veggies becoming pink from the beet juice, you can cook all the vegetables together.) Reduce the heat under both pots to medium. Cook the sweet potato, carrot and parsnip for 4 to 5 minutes, then drain them and rinse them with cold water immediately to prevent them from cooking further. Cook the beets for 10 to 12 minutes, until they are tender. Rinse the beets separately from the other vegetables to prevent them from turning pink.

While the vegetables are cooking, take the puff pastry out of the freezer and let it thaw. Preheat the oven to 350°F (175°C). Grease a 9-inch (23-cm) tart pan with a removable bottom.

To continue preparing the thyme cashew mozzarella, add the water, nutritional yeast, tapioca flour, garlic, salt and black pepper to the blender and blend for 1 to 2 minutes, until the mixture is smooth. Pour the mixture into a medium saucepan over medium heat and add the thyme. Stir continuously for 4 to 5 minutes to avoid clumping, until the mozzarella reaches a thick and stretchy consistency. Take the saucepan off the heat and set it aside.

(continued)

GLAZE

1 tbsp (15 ml) pure maple syrup

1 tbsp (12 g) coconut sugar

1 tbsp (14 g) vegan butter

1 tbsp (15 ml) white wine vinegar

CANDIED NUTS

1 tbsp (14 g) vegan butter

1 tbsp (12 g) coconut sugar

½ cup (60 g) walnuts

To make the glaze, combine the syrup, sugar, butter and vinegar in a small saucepan over high heat and boil the mixture for 1 to 2 minutes, until the sugar has melted.

Place the puff pastry in the prepared tart pan, trimming the edges and pressing down on the bottom and sides. Spoon the mozzarella into the pastry and spread it out evenly. Cut the root vegetables into thin slices and layer them on top of the mozzarella. Carefully brush the top of the veggies with the glaze and place the tart in the oven. Bake for 25 minutes, until the pastry is golden brown.

In the meantime, prepare the candied nuts. In a small saucepan over medium heat, melt the butter and sugar together. Add the walnuts and stir until they are evenly coated. Set the nuts aside and let them cool. Sprinkle the nuts on top of the baked tart and add extra thyme leaves before serving.

CHICKPEA LOAF WITH BALSAMIC GLAZE

This hearty loaf of chickpeas, nuts and vegetables is pure deliciousness! Speckled with colorful bits of carrot and celery and brushed with a tangy balsamic glaze, it's as savory as it is satisfying. Serve it with a side of salad, mashed potatoes or roasted cauliflower and you have the perfect dish for any occasion. • **GLUTEN FREE** •

YIELD: 10 servings

CHICKPEA LOAF

1 cup (165 g) cooked chickpeas, drained and rinsed

1 cup (140 g) raw almonds

2 tbsp (20 g) flaxseeds

½ cup (45 g) rolled oats (gluten free, if needed)

1 cup (140 g) cooked chestnuts, finely chopped

1 tsp fresh thyme leaves, finely chopped

Pinch of ground nutmeg

1 tbsp (15 ml) balsamic vinegar

Salt, to taste

Black pepper, to taste

2 tbsp (30 ml) olive oil

1 medium red onion, finely chopped

2 medium ribs celery, finely chopped

1 medium carrot, finely chopped

2 cups (150 g) finely chopped portobello mushrooms

⅓ cup (80 ml) vegetable broth

2 cloves garlic, minced

BALSAMIC GLAZE

2 tbsp (30 ml) balsamic vinegar

1 tbsp (8 g) cornstarch

½ cup (120 ml) vegetable broth

¼ cup (60 ml) tomato passata

2 to 3 tbsp (30 to 45 ml) date syrup or molasses

To make the chickpea loaf, place the chickpeas in a large bowl and mash them with a potato masher, leaving only a few chunks. Combine the almonds, flaxseeds and oats in a food processor and pulse a few times until the ingredients achieve a flour-like consistency. Add the almond mixture to the chickpeas. Add the chestnuts, thyme, nutmeg, vinegar, salt and black pepper and combine.

Heat the olive oil in a large saucepan over medium heat. Add the onion and celery and sauté for 3 minutes, until they are translucent. Add the carrot, mushrooms, broth and garlic and cook for 6 to 8 minutes, until the vegetables are soft. Add the vegetables to the chickpeas and combine.

Preheat the oven to 350°F (175°C) and line a 9 x 5–inch (23 x 13–cm) loaf pan with parchment paper. Spoon the chickpea mixture into the loaf pan and press down evenly with a spoon. Set the chickpea loaf aside.

To make the balsamic glaze, combine the vinegar and cornstarch in a small saucepan and mix well. Add the broth, tomato passata and syrup and bring the mixture to a boil over medium heat. Let the glaze simmer for 3 to 4 minutes, until it has thickened, then take the saucepan off the heat. Brush the top of the chickpea loaf with the glaze (reserving the rest of the glaze for serving) and bake the loaf for 60 minutes. Let the loaf rest for 10 minutes before slicing.

HEARTY SHEPHERD'S PIE

This vegan version of the British classic is everything I'm craving on a cold winter night. It's warm, comforting, packed with nutrients, super easy to whip up and bursting with flavor. It's the ideal centerpiece on any holiday or weeknight table. • **GLUTEN FREE** •

YIELD: 8 servings

POTATO MASH

5 large white potatoes, peeled and cubed

¼ cup (60 ml) soy milk

1 tbsp (14 g) vegan butter

½ tsp salt

¼ tsp black pepper

1 tbsp (3 g) fresh thyme leaves, plus more as needed

VEGETABLE FILLING

2 tbsp (30 ml) olive oil

1 medium white onion, finely chopped

3 cloves garlic, minced

½ tsp ground cinnamon

¼ tsp ground nutmeg

1 tbsp (3 g) dried oregano

2 tbsp (28 g) tomato paste

1 tbsp (15 ml) red wine

1 tbsp (15 ml) soy sauce

1 medium carrot, finely chopped

2 medium ribs celery, finely chopped

4 cremini mushrooms, thickly sliced

2 cups (480 ml) vegetable broth, divided

1 (14-oz [400-g]) can lentils, drained and rinsed

Preheat the oven to 400°F (200°C).

To make the potato mash, fill a large pot with water and bring the water to a boil over high heat. Add the potatoes, reduce the heat to medium and cook until they are tender, 15 to 20 minutes. Drain the potatoes and mash them in the pot along with the milk, butter, salt, black pepper and thyme until the mash is rich and creamy. Set the potato mash aside.

To make the vegetable filling, heat the oil in a large saucepan over medium-high heat. Add the onion and cook for 3 minutes, until it is translucent. Add the garlic, cinnamon, nutmeg, oregano, tomato paste, wine and soy sauce. Stir until the onion and garlic are well coated by the spices, then reduce the heat to low and cook for 2 minutes.

Increase the heat to medium. Add the carrot, celery, mushrooms and ½ cup (120 ml) of the broth and stir until combined. Cover the saucepan and cook the mixture for 5 minutes. Add the lentils and remaining 1½ cups (360 ml) of broth and simmer, uncovered, for 10 to 15 minutes, stirring occasionally, until the liquid is absorbed and the mixture is thick.

Transfer the vegetable filling to a 7 x 10–inch (18 x 25–cm) baking dish and spread it out evenly with a spatula. Carefully scoop the potato mash on top of the filling and flatten it out. At this point, you can use a fork or spoon to carve marks into the mash if desired. Spray the top of the shepherd's pie with cooking spray and bake it for 25 minutes, until the mash is golden brown on top. Garnish with additional thyme and serve.

GLUTEN-FREE SUBSTITUTE: Use tamari sauce, a type of soy sauce that is traditionally made without wheat.

MISO-TAHINI ROASTED CAULIFLOWER

As a vegan-friendly twist to the traditional holiday roast, this cauliflower is the ultimate warming side or main dish. Cauliflower is such an underrated vegetable that it is about time we give it a new, Asian-inspired makeover! Covered in a thick crust of delicious miso-tahini sauce, this beauty will truly impress. • **GLUTEN FREE** •

YIELD: 4 servings

CAULIFLOWER

1 medium head cauliflower

2 tbsp (6 g) fresh parsley, finely chopped

Salt, to taste

MISO-TAHINI SAUCE

2 tbsp (30 g) tahini

1 tsp brown rice miso

1 tsp fresh lemon juice

1 tsp date syrup

4 to 5 tbsp (60 to 75 ml) water

Preheat the oven to 400°F (200°C). Line a small baking sheet with parchment paper.

To prepare the cauliflower, wash the cauliflower and trim the leaves so that the cauliflower head stands up straight. Fill a large pot three-quarters full of water and bring it to a boil over high heat. Once the water is boiling, carefully add the cauliflower head and reduce the heat to medium. Simmer the cauliflower for 10 to 12 minutes, until it is tender, and drain.

To make the miso-tahini sauce, combine the tahini, miso, lemon juice, syrup and water in a small bowl, using more water for a thinner sauce and less for a thicker sauce.

Place the cauliflower on the prepared baking sheet and gently brush half of the miso-tahini sauce on the top and sides of the cauliflower. Bake the cauliflower for 7 minutes. Take the cauliflower out of the oven and gently brush the remaining sauce on the top and sides. Bake for 7 to 10 minutes, until the cauliflower is golden brown on top. Serve the cauliflower sprinkled with the parsley and salt.

MUSHROOM BOURGUIGNON

Bourguignon is a traditional French recipe made with Burgundy or red wine. This vegan mushroom bourguignon keeps the strong, authentic flavors while offering a healthier, plant-based alternative to this comforting meal! It is best served with mashed potatoes (page 20).

YIELD: 4 servings

2 tbsp (30 ml) olive oil

1 medium white onion, diced

2 tbsp (28 g) tomato paste

16 oz (450 g) cremini mushrooms, thinly sliced

1 medium carrot, diced

1 medium orange bell pepper, diced

1 tbsp (3 g) fresh thyme leaves

2 cloves garlic, minced

½ cup (120 ml) water

2 tbsp (30 ml) soy sauce

¾ cup (180 ml) dry red wine

1 tbsp (14 g) vegan butter, softened

2 tbsp (16 g) all-purpose flour

Salt, to taste

Black pepper, to taste

Potato Mash (page 20)

Heat the olive oil in a large pot over medium heat. Add the onion and sauté for 3 to 5 minutes, until it is golden brown. Add the tomato paste, mushrooms, carrot, bell pepper, thyme and garlic and cook for 5 to 10 minutes. Add the water, soy sauce and wine and cook for 10 minutes, until the liquid has reduced and the vegetables are soft.

In a small bowl, mash together the butter and flour with a fork. Add this mixture to the pot and stir continuously until the sauce thickens, 3 to 4 minutes. Season the mixture with the salt and black pepper and serve on top of the mashed potatoes.

GLUTEN-FREE SUBSTITUTE: To make this recipe gluten free, use tamari sauce, a type of soy sauce that is traditionally made without wheat, and use a gluten-free all-purpose flour blend (Bob's Red Mill has a great one). You'll usually need a bit extra: 1 to 2 tablespoons (6 to 12 g) per 1 cup (90 g) of flour.

SPICED-APPLE RED CABBAGE

This beautiful and warmly spiced red cabbage accompanied me through every single Christmas celebration while I was growing up. It's a very traditional and festive side dish in Germany, and I've been looking forward to eating a bowl of this deliciousness once a year for as long as I can remember. My mum was kind enough to share our family's traditional recipe so more people can enjoy the glory of Spiced-Apple Red Cabbage. • **GLUTEN FREE** •

YIELD: 4 servings

1 medium head red cabbage, sliced

2 tbsp (24 g) coconut sugar

¼ tsp salt

1 cup (240 ml) red wine

⅓ cup (80 ml) balsamic vinegar

3 dried bay leaves

¼ tsp ground ginger

¼ tsp ground cloves

2 tbsp (30 ml) olive oil

1 medium white onion, diced

4 tbsp (60 g) unsweetened applesauce

1 (2-inch [5-cm]) cinnamon stick

Take off the outer leaves of the red cabbage. Cut off the stem end, core the cabbage and slice it into thin strips (for a finer texture, you could also grate it). Transfer the cabbage to a large bowl. Add the sugar and salt and massage the cabbage for 3 minutes, until it's evenly coated. Add the wine, vinegar, bay leaves, ginger and cloves and combine. Cover the bowl loosely with a towel and let the cabbage rest for 2 hours.

Heat the oil in a large pot over medium heat. Add the onion and sauté until it is translucent, 3 to 4 minutes. Add the cabbage, along with the liquid in the bowl. Add the applesauce and cinnamon stick and cook, covered, for 20 minutes. Uncover the pot and cook for 40 minutes, stirring frequently.

Remove and discard the bay leaves and cinnamon stick and place the cabbage in a serving bowl.

QUICK TIP: This festive recipe is ideal to prepare a day or two ahead of time in order to avoid spending hours in the kitchen on a busy holiday. In my opinion, it actually gets better after a day in the fridge as the spices integrate even more with the cabbage!

MAPLE-ROASTED BRUSSELS SPROUTS WITH PEAR

Brussels sprouts seem like a holiday no-brainer, yet they can be easily overlooked. These roasted Brussels sprouts are an easy and flavorful recipe that highlight fall and winter's freshest ingredients. They are a quintessential side dish to any holiday meal, with a subtle sweetness and exciting crunch! • **GLUTEN FREE** •

YIELD: 4 servings

17½ oz (490 g) Brussels sprouts, trimmed and sliced in half

1 medium red onion, thinly sliced

1 medium pear (any variety), diced

1 tbsp (3 g) fresh thyme leaves, plus more as needed

2 tbsp (30 ml) pure maple syrup

2 tbsp (30 ml) olive oil

¼ tsp salt

Dash of black pepper

1 tbsp (9 g) raw almonds, roughly chopped

1 tsp fresh lemon juice

Preheat the oven to 400°F (200°C) and line a medium baking sheet with parchment paper.

On the prepared baking sheet, combine the Brussels sprouts, onion, pear, thyme, maple syrup, oil, salt and black pepper, spreading the mixture out evenly and coating it in the oil and spices.

Roast the Brussels sprouts on the oven's center rack for 20 to 25 minutes, rotating the pan halfway through. Add the almonds during the last 5 to 7 minutes, roasting until they are toasted. Drizzle the lemon juice on top, garnish with extra thyme and serve immediately.

GREEN BEANS WITH CARAMELIZED ONIONS

These fresh green beans with caramelized onions offer a lighter and healthier alternative to go along with all the other rich, melt-in-your-mouth dishes on your holiday table. They are ready in no time and the perfect crunchy addition to your feast! • **GLUTEN FREE** •

YIELD: 4 servings

2 lb (900 g) fresh green beans, trimmed and washed

1 tbsp (15 ml) olive oil

1 tbsp (14 g) vegan butter

1 medium red onion, thickly sliced

1 clove garlic, minced

½ tsp salt, or to taste

¼ tsp ground black pepper

1 tsp lemon zest

3 tbsp (18 g) sliced, blanched almonds

Bring a large pot of salted water to a boil over high heat. Add the green beans, reduce the heat to medium, cook for 2 to 4 minutes (depending on how crunchy you like them), then drain.

Combine the oil and butter in a large skillet over high heat. Add the onion and sauté for 3 to 4 minutes, until it is translucent and caramelized. Add the garlic and cook for 1 minute, then add the green beans and cook until they reach the desired level of doneness. Season with the salt and black pepper and serve with the lemon zest and sliced almonds on top.

ONION DUMPLINGS

These vegan onion dumplings are not only easy to assemble but are also super fun to make for a family get-together! Dumplings are widespread across many cultures, but these onion dumplings are inspired by traditional Eastern European cuisine. When it comes to Christmas dumplings, it's all about the filling, which can vary from caramelized onions to spiced cabbage or even a sweet cinnamon-apple mixture. To make these extra festive, switch the Asian-style dipping sauce for a spiced cranberry dip!

YIELD: 20 dumplings

DOUGH

1 ½ cups (180 g) all-purpose flour

¼ tsp salt

½ cup (120 ml) hot water

FILLING

1 tbsp (15 ml) olive oil

1 large yellow onion, diced

1 clove garlic, minced

3 to 4 cremini mushrooms, thinly sliced

3 leaves of white cabbage, thinly sliced

¼ cup (12 g) thinly sliced green onions

1 tbsp (15 ml) soy sauce

Salt, to taste

Black pepper, to taste

To prepare the dough, combine the flour and salt in a large bowl. Add the water and use an electric hand mixer fitted with a dough hook to combine until a crumbly dough forms. Transfer the dough to a floured work surface and knead for 8 to 10 minutes, until the dough is smooth. Wrap the dough in plastic wrap and let it stand for 45 minutes.

Unwrap the dough, knead it again for 5 minutes, wrap it again and let it stand for 30 minutes. After 30 minutes, it should be springy and soft.

While the dough rests, prepare the filling. Heat the olive oil in a large saucepan over medium heat. Add the onion and sauté for 3 to 4 minutes, until it is translucent. Add the garlic, mushrooms, cabbage, green onions and soy sauce and cook for 5 to 6 minutes, until the vegetables are soft. Season the filling with the salt and black pepper.

(continued)

CRANBERRY DIPPING SAUCE

4 tbsp (80 g) cranberry sauce

1 tbsp (15 ml) apple cider vinegar

1 tbsp (15 ml) water

1 tsp soy sauce

½ tsp ground cinnamon

SOY SAUCE DIPPING SAUCE

3 tbsp (45 ml) soy sauce

½ tsp light or dark sesame oil

½ tsp garlic powder

¼ tsp red pepper flakes

DUMPLINGS

3 to 4 tbsp (30 to 40 g) sesame seeds

1 tbsp (15 ml) olive oil

½ cup (120 ml) water

To make the cranberry dipping sauce, whisk together the cranberry sauce, vinegar, water, soy sauce and cinnamon in a small bowl and set aside.

To make the soy sauce dipping sauce, whisk together the soy sauce, oil, garlic powder and red pepper flakes in a small bowl and set aside.

Flour a work surface. Next to the floured area, place a shallow bowl of water. Place the sesame seeds on a plate and place it next to the bowl of water.

Divide the dough into 8 pieces and roll each piece into 1-inch (2.5-cm)-thick ropes on the floured work surface. Cut the ropes into 20 pieces and roll out each piece into 3½-inch (8.75-cm) circles. Spoon 1 tablespoon (15 g) of the filling onto the center of each circle wrapper. Bring up the sides of the wrapper, press and pleat the edges to seal in the filling, then twist the seal clockwise about 45 degrees.

To prepare the dumplings, dip the bottom of each stuffed, sealed dough wrapper into the bowl of water, then dip it into sesame seeds until the bottom is covered.

Heat the oil in a large skillet over medium heat and arrange the dumplings in the skillet, with the sesame seeds facing downward. Cook for 1 minute, then add the water and cover the skillet. Steam the dumplings for 5 minutes. Uncover the skillet and cook until the bottoms of the dumplings are golden brown, 1 to 2 minutes, then transfer them to a platter and serve with either or both of the dipping sauces.

CHOCOLATE YULE LOG

Christmas wouldn't be Christmas without a proper Yule log. This recipe creates a perfectly decadent, spongy vegan Yule log filled with a silky smooth cream and coated in a scrumptious chocolate ganache. Are you drooling yet?

YIELD: 10 servings

CHOCOLATE SPONGE CAKE

1½ cups (180 g) all-purpose flour

1 tbsp (8 g) cornstarch

¼ cup (48 g) coconut sugar

2 tbsp (14 g) cacao powder

½ tsp baking powder

½ tsp baking soda

Pinch of salt

1 cup plus 2 tbsp (270 ml) almond or soy milk

1 tsp apple cider vinegar

2 tbsp (30 ml) melted coconut oil

2 tbsp (30 g) unsweetened applesauce

CREAM FILLING

1 (14-oz [420-ml]) can full-fat coconut cream, refrigerated overnight

1 tbsp (15 ml) pure maple syrup

1 tsp pure vanilla extract

To make the chocolate sponge cake, preheat the oven to 350°F (175°C) and line a rimmed 9½ x 12½–inch (24 x 31.75–cm) baking sheet with parchment paper, making sure the edges are completely covered. (Note that it's important to use a baking sheet that's close to these dimensions, or the cake will be too thick or thin to roll.)

In large bowl, combine the flour, cornstarch, coconut sugar, cacao powder, baking powder, baking soda and salt. In a medium bowl, combine the milk, vinegar, oil and applesauce. Pour the milk mixture into the flour mixture and stir until just combined. The batter should be thick and pourable.

Transfer the batter to the prepared baking sheet and spread it into an even layer about a ½ inch (13 mm) thick. Bake the cake for 10 to 12 minutes, or until a toothpick inserted into the center comes out clean. Let the cake cool for 2 minutes.

Gently roll the cake from short end to short end, rolling the parchment paper up inside the cake and using it as a guide. Be very careful during this step so as not to break the cake—try to handle it as little as possible. Let the rolled cake cool to room temperature (otherwise the filling will melt).

While the cake is cooling, make the cream filling. Scoop only the solid portion of the chilled coconut cream into a medium bowl, then add the maple syrup and vanilla. Whip the cream filling using a hand mixer until it is light and fluffy, 1 to 2 minutes. Place the cream filling in the fridge for 30 minutes.

(continued)

CHOCOLATE GANACHE

⅓ cup (75 g) vegan butter

½ cup (56 g) cacao powder

1 cup (130 g) powdered sugar, plus more as needed

1 tbsp (15 ml) almond or soy milk

To make the chocolate ganache, combine the butter, cacao powder, powdered sugar and milk in a medium bowl. Whip the ganache using a hand mixer until it is smooth, 1 to 2 minutes. Place the ganache in the fridge for 30 minutes.

Once the cake has cooled to room temperature, carefully unroll it and top it with all of the cream filling. Spread the filling evenly over the cake, leaving a ½-inch (13-mm) border along the edges. Begin rolling the cake back up the same way it was unrolled, from short end to short end, removing the parchment paper as you go. Continue rolling, using the parchment paper as a guide, until the cake is seam-side down. Wipe away any excess filling that may have spilled over.

Gently wrap the cake in parchment paper and carefully transfer it to a cutting board. Place the cutting board in the refrigerator until the cake is completely chilled and firm enough to handle easily, 30 to 60 minutes. Carefully unroll it from the parchment wrap and place it on a serving platter.

Spread the chocolate ganache on top of the cake and use a frosting knife to shape the cake like a wooden log. Leave the Yule log as is or dust it with a bit of powdered sugar. Use a clean knife to carefully slice the log into pieces. Store leftovers covered in the refrigerator for 3 to 4 days.

DECADENT VEGAN TIRAMISU

Who doesn't love tiramisu? Layers upon layers of delicious, coffee-soaked, spongy cake filled with mascarpone and lots of cacao powder. This vegan version is absolutely heavenly and one of my favorite festive desserts because it's so rich yet easy to make! • **GLUTEN FREE** •

YIELD: 4 servings

MASCARPONE

¾ cup (115 g) raw cashews

1 (14-oz [420-ml]) can full-fat coconut cream, refrigerated overnight

1 tsp pure vanilla extract

2 tbsp (30 ml) pure maple syrup

3 tbsp (45 ml) melted coconut oil

Pinch of salt

¼ cup (60 ml) almond milk

VANILLA SPONGE CAKE

½ cup (120 ml) almond milk

1 tsp apple cider vinegar

1 tbsp (15 ml) melted coconut oil

1 tsp pure vanilla extract

1 cup (96 g) almond flour

¼ cup (23 g) gluten-free or (30 g) regular all-purpose flour

1 tbsp (8 g) cornstarch

½ tsp baking powder

¼ tsp baking soda

¼ cup (48 g) coconut sugar

Pinch of salt

To begin preparing the mascarpone, place the cashews in a medium bowl and cover them with water. Let them soak for 6 to 8 hours (or overnight), then drain them and place them in a high-speed blender.

To begin preparing the vanilla sponge cake, preheat the oven to 350°F (175°C) and line an 8 x 8–inch (20 x 20–cm) baking pan with parchment paper.

In a medium bowl, combine the almond milk and vinegar and let the milk curdle for 5 minutes to achieve vegan buttermilk. Add the oil and vanilla and combine.

In a large bowl, combine the almond flour, all-purpose flour, cornstarch, baking powder, baking soda, sugar and salt and whisk together. Pour the milk mixture into the flour mixture and stir just enough to form a batter (don't overmix). Pour the batter into the baking pan and bake the cake for 10 minutes, until a toothpick inserted into the center comes out clean.

(continued)

COFFEE SYRUP

½ cup (120 ml) freshly brewed coffee

2 tbsp (24 g) coconut sugar

2 tbsp (30 ml) amaretto or spiced rum (optional)

TOPPING

Cacao powder, for dusting

To make the coffee syrup, combine the coffee, sugar and amaretto (if using) in a small bowl and stir until the sugar has dissolved. Set aside and let the coffee cool.

To finish preparing the mascarpone, scoop only the solid portion of the chilled coconut cream into the blender. Add the vanilla, maple syrup, coconut oil and salt to the blender and blend on high for 1 to 2 minutes, until the mixture is smooth. Transfer half of the filling to a medium bowl. Add ¼ cup (60 ml) of the coffee syrup and whisk to combine. Add the milk to the blender and blend again until the mixture is smooth.

To assemble the tiramisu, cut out a piece of the vanilla sponge cake and place in the bottom of each of 4 serving glasses. Add 1 tablespoon (15 ml) of the coffee syrup on top and let it soak in for a few seconds. Top the cake with a layer of the mascarpone, dust the mascarpone with the cacao powder and place the serving glasses in the freezer for 10 minutes. Top each serving with a layer of the coffee mascarpone then a layer of cacao powder and return the tiramisu to the freezer for 10 minutes.

Crumble the remaining vanilla sponge cake on top of each serving and repeat the preceding layering steps, freezing for 10 minutes in between until all the ingredients have been used. Once the tiramisu is finished, dust the top with more cacao powder and transfer each serving to the fridge to set for 3 to 4 hours before serving.

BAKED APPLES WITH VANILLA ICE CREAM

Winter wouldn't be winter without the smell of freshly baked apples and cinnamon throughout the house. With a heavenly spiced filling made of toasted nuts, marzipan and rum-soaked raisins, these apples are a must-have for Christmas fans—especially with a dollop of homemade vegan vanilla ice cream on top! • GLUTEN FREE •

YIELD: 4 servings

VANILLA ICE CREAM

2 (14-oz [420-ml]) cans full-fat coconut cream, refrigerated overnight

¾ cup (180 ml) cashew or almond milk

⅓ cup (80 ml) pure maple syrup

1 tsp pure vanilla extract

½ tsp vanilla powder

Pinch of salt

BAKED APPLES

⅓ cup (50 g) raisins

¼ cup (60 ml) rum (optional)

4 medium apples (any variety)

Juice and zest from ½ organic lemon

2 tbsp (28 g) vegan butter

¼ cup (28 g) slivered almonds

¼ cup (43 g) hazelnuts, finely chopped

½ tsp ground cinnamon

4 (2-inch [5-cm]) cinnamon sticks

To make the vanilla ice cream, scoop only the solid portion of the chilled coconut cream into a medium saucepan. Add the milk and heat the mixture over medium heat. Whisk for 1 to 2 minutes, until the coconut cream has melted. Remove the saucepan from the heat and stir in the syrup, vanilla extract, vanilla powder and salt.

Transfer the ice cream mixture to a glass bowl and refrigerate until the mixture has cooled. Once the mixture is chilled, pour it into the bowl of an ice cream machine and mix according to the manufacturer's instructions. This will take anywhere from 30 to 45 minutes. When the ice cream machine stops, transfer the ice cream to a freezer-safe container and put it in the freezer.

To make the baked apples, combine the raisins and rum (if using) in a small bowl and let them soak for 15 minutes. (If you are not using the rum, simply skip this step and add the raisins when they are called for later in the directions.)

In the meantime, cut off the tops of the apples (reserving them for later). Remove their stems and carefully scoop out the insides of the apples, leaving a 1-inch (2.5-cm) border. Brush the insides of the apples with the lemon juice to prevent browning.

Preheat the oven to 350°F (175°C) and line a 7 x 10–inch (18 x 25–cm) baking dish with parchment paper.

(continued)

MARZIPAN

½ cup (48 g) almond flour

¼ cup (33 g) powdered sugar

1 tsp almond extract

1 tbsp (15 ml) pure maple syrup

While the oven preheats, prepare the marzipan. Place the flour, powdered sugar, almond extract and maple syrup in a food processor and pulse until a sticky mass forms. Set aside.

Heat the butter in a small saucepan over medium heat until it is melted. Add the almonds and hazelnuts and toast for 1 minute. Add the sticky marzipan, ground cinnamon, raisins and lemon zest and cook for 1 to 2 minutes. Divide the filling between the apples. Add the tops of the apples and place the stuffed apples in the prepared baking dish. Bake for 20 to 25 minutes, then remove the apples and let them cool down slightly.

Serve the baked apples with a scoop of vanilla ice cream and a cinnamon stick for decoration.

HAZELNUT CHRISTMAS TREE

This is the perfect sweet for your Christmas festivities! It's incredibly easy to make and a great dessert to nibble on after an indulgent meal. Filled with homemade vegan chocolate-hazelnut spread, this delightful treat will surely bring a smile to your guests' faces.

YIELD: 10 servings

CHOCOLATE-HAZELNUT SPREAD

1 cup (170 g) roasted hazelnuts, without skins

3 oz (84 g) 70% cacao vegan dark chocolate, melted

½ cup (120 ml) full-fat coconut cream, plus more as needed

2 tbsp (30 ml) pure maple syrup

CHRISTMAS TREE

2 sheets vegan puff pastry, partially thawed

1 tbsp (15 ml) neutral-flavored oil (e.g., sunflower oil)

To make the chocolate-hazelnut spread, place the hazelnuts, chocolate, cream and maple syrup in a high-speed blender and blend until smooth. Spoon the spread into a jar and store any leftovers in the fridge.

To make the Christmas tree, preheat the oven to 350°F (175°C) and line a large baking sheet with parchment paper.

Place the first sheet of puff pastry on the prepared baking sheet and cut out a triangle with a tree stump shape at the bottom. Spoon the chocolate-hazelnut on top and spread it out evenly. Place the second sheet of puff pastry on top, press down slightly and trim away the excess pastry.

Moving outward, make even cuts down both sides of the triangle, leaving 1 inch (2.5 cm) uncut in the center to keep the tree together. Twist each cut strip from top to bottom to create the tree branches. Brush the top of the pastry with the oil and bake for 10 to 15 minutes, until the pastry is well risen and golden brown.

Blend any leftover chocolate-hazelnut spread with more coconut cream for a smooth dipping sauce and serve.

SPECULOOS COOKIE CUPCAKES

These cookie butter cupcakes are the definition of a holiday treat! If you're not familiar with the speculoos cookie, you have missed out. It's a type of spiced short-crust cookie bursting with festive spices such as cinnamon, ginger, cloves, cardamom and nutmeg—the perfect flavor combo to use in this light and fluffy cupcake that is completely egg free and topped with an indulgent speculoos cookie butter frosting, which brings out those gingerbread flavors to the fullest.

YIELD: 6 cupcakes

CUPCAKES

½ cup (120 ml) almond or soy milk

1 tsp apple cider vinegar

3 tbsp (45 ml) melted coconut oil

1 tbsp (16 g) cookie butter spread, melted

¼ cup (60 ml) pure maple syrup

½ tsp pure vanilla extract

1 cup (115 g) spelt flour

½ tsp baking powder

½ tsp baking soda

Pinch of salt

3 speculoos cookies

FROSTING

3 tbsp (42 g) vegan butter

⅓ cup (85 g) cookie butter spread

½ cup (65 g) powdered sugar

Preheat the oven to 350°F (175°C) and line a 12-cup muffin pan with 6 cupcake liners.

To make the cupcakes, combine the milk with the vinegar in a medium bowl. Let the milk curdle for 5 minutes to achieve vegan buttermilk. Add the melted oil, cookie butter, maple syrup and vanilla and stir to combine.

In a large bowl, combine the flour, baking powder, baking soda and salt and whisk together. Pour the milk mixture into the flour mixture and stir just enough to form a batter (don't overmix). Fill each cupcake liner two-thirds full and bake the cupcakes for 10 to 12 minutes, until a toothpick inserted into the center comes out clean. Remove the cupcakes from the oven and place them on a wire rack to cool.

In the meantime, make the frosting. In a medium bowl, combine the butter, cookie butter spread and powdered sugar. Beat the ingredients with an electric hand mixer until they form a smooth frosting. Scoop the frosting into a piping bag and frost the cupcakes once they have cooled down. Top each cupcake with half a cookie and transfer the cupcakes to a serving platter.

RAFFAELLO-STYLE TRUFFLES

These raw vegan truffles are a healthier version of the name-brand candy that don't sacrifice the flavor. If you're not familiar with Raffaello, they're a very popular European treat that consists of an almond surrounded by rich coconut cream and coated in desiccated coconut. These coconutty truffles make the perfect Christmas treat or edible present, with no guilt involved whatsoever! • **GLUTEN FREE** •

YIELD: 12 truffles

⅓ cup (75 g) coconut butter

2 tbsp (28 g) solid chilled coconut cream

1 tbsp (15 ml) pure maple syrup

¼ tsp vanilla powder or pure vanilla extract

3 tbsp plus ⅓ cup (40 g) desiccated coconut, divided

12 blanched almonds

To make the truffles, melt the coconut butter and coconut cream in a small saucepan over medium heat. Take the saucepan off the heat and transfer the coconut butter mixture to a small bowl. Add the maple syrup, vanilla and 3 tablespoons (15 g) of the desiccated coconut and combine. Place the mixture in the fridge for 1 hour, until it's firm.

Place the remaining ⅓ cup (25 g) of desiccated coconut in a shallow dish. Use a melon baller to form small truffles from the chilled mixture and roll them in your hands until you have the desired shape. Place an almond in the middle of each ball, then roll it around in the remaining desiccated coconut until it is covered. Store the truffles in the fridge until ready to serve.

CHOCOLATE-HAZELNUT TRUFFLES

A healthier, vegan take on the popular Ferrero Rocher candy shouldn't be missing this Christmas! I have very fond memories of finding these little balls of heaven on my "sweet plate" under the Christmas tree every single year when I was growing up. They're also the perfect gift to surprise loved ones with, so make sure to double the recipe—just in case! • **GLUTEN FREE** •

YIELD: 15 truffles

5.6 oz (157 g) 70% cacao vegan dark chocolate

½ cup (120 ml) full-fat coconut milk

3 to 4 tbsp (45 to 60 ml) pure maple syrup

½ cup (90 g) hazelnut butter (see Quick Tip)

½ cup (58 g) finely chopped roasted hazelnuts

½ cup (85 g) whole roasted hazelnuts

Place the chocolate in a small glass bowl. Bring a small pot partially filled with water to a simmer over medium-low heat. Place the glass bowl in the pot, making sure the bowl does not actually touch the simmering water. Heat the chocolate until it is melted and smooth, 3 to 4 minutes. Take the pot and bowl off the heat but leave the bowl sitting over the warm water bath. Add the milk a little at a time and whisk until smooth. If the chocolate seizes (that is, becomes grainy and hard), don't worry. Just keep adding milk and whisking at the same time. Eventually the chocolate will return to its smooth state. Add the maple syrup and hazelnut butter and stir until combined.

Place the bowl in the freezer for a minimum of 2 hours, or until the chocolate is firm. Place the chopped hazelnuts in a shallow dish. Line a small baking sheet with parchment paper.

Once the chocolate is firm, scoop out some of the mixture and roll it in your hands into a small truffle. Take a whole hazelnut and press it into the center of the truffle. Finally, roll the truffle in the chopped hazelnuts until it is completely covered and place it on the prepared baking sheet. Repeat this step until the chocolate mixture is gone. Place the baking sheet in the freezer for 30 minutes.

Let the truffles defrost at room temperature for 5 minutes before serving. Store them in the freezer for up to 1 month.

QUICK TIP: If you can't find store-bought hazelnut butter, you can easily make it at home. Preheat the oven to 350°F (175°C) and line a medium baking sheet with parchment paper. Spread 2 cups (340 g) of hazelnuts out on the baking sheet in an even layer. Roast the hazelnuts for 10 to 12 minutes, until golden brown. Let them cool slightly, transfer them to a kitchen towel and rub them with the towel to remove the skins. Place the hazelnuts in a food processor or high-speed blender and blend on low for 7 to 9 minutes, scraping down the sides as needed, until the nuts become a creamy, smooth butter.

FESTIVE GINGERBREAD COOKIES

'Tis the season for warming spices and boxes full of delicious cookies—the more the merrier! This spicy cookie is perfect for making gingerbread men. I usually roll the dough out a bit thicker than usual, just to give the cookies a hint of chew. If you're planning to whip up a batch of gingerbread cookies over the holiday, I've got just the recipe for you.

YIELD: 20 cookies

COOKIES

1 tbsp (7 g) ground flaxseed

3 tbsp (45 ml) water

1 cup (130 g) whole wheat flour

½ cup (60 g) all-purpose flour

⅓ cup (48 g) brown sugar

½ tsp baking soda

Pinch of salt

1 tsp ground cinnamon

1 tsp ground ginger

¼ tsp ground cloves

¼ tsp ground nutmeg

4 tbsp (56 g) vegan butter

4 tbsp (60 ml) molasses

ICING

¼ cup (33 g) powdered sugar

½ lsp pure vanilla extract

½ tsp almond or soy milk

To make the cookies, combine the flaxseed and water in a small bowl to create a flax egg. Set aside and let the mixture thicken.

In the meantime, combine the whole wheat flour, all-purpose flour, brown sugar, baking soda, salt, cinnamon, ginger, cloves and nutmeg in a large bowl and whisk together. Add the butter, molasses and flax egg and mix with an electric hand mixer fitted with kneading hooks for 3 minutes, until a crumbly dough forms. Using your hands, knead the dough for 1 minute until you have a smooth ball. Wrap it in plastic wrap and place it in the fridge for 30 minutes.

Meanwhile, preheat the oven to 350°F (175°C) and line a large baking sheet with parchment paper.

Place the dough on a floured work surface, roll it out about ⅛ inch (3 mm) thick and cut out gingerbread men with cookie cutters. Place the cookies on the prepared baking sheet and bake for 8 to 10 minutes on the oven's center rack. They will look underdone but will firm up as they cool; this is crucial for soft cookies.

Remove the cookies from the oven and let them rest for 5 minutes before transferring them to a wire rack to cool completely.

While the cookies are cooling, prepare the icing. In a small bowl, whisk together the powdered sugar, vanilla and milk until a smooth icing forms. Once the cookies are completely cool, pipe on the icing.

CHOCOLATE REINDEER COOKIES

The Christmas season is all about spending quality time with your family and creating the cutest winter-theme treats. These adorable Chocolate Reindeer Cookies are super simple to make and would be great for any Christmas party.

YIELD: 12 cookies

GOOGLY EYES

¼ cup (33 g) powdered sugar

¼ tsp cornstarch

1 tsp almond milk

15 to 20 70% cacao vegan mini dark chocolate chips

REINDEER COOKIES

½ cup (60 g) all-purpose flour

⅓ cup (64 g) coconut sugar

¼ tsp baking soda

¼ tsp salt

¼ cup (60 ml) melted coconut oil

½ cup (90 g) peanut butter

2 tbsp (30 ml) almond milk

½ tsp pure vanilla extract

¼ cup (45 g) 70% cacao vegan dark chocolate chips

FROSTING

⅓ cup (60 g) peanut butter

1 tbsp (15 ml) pure maple syrup

1 to 2 tbsp (15 to 30 ml) almond milk

2 tbsp (14 g) cacao powder

EARS AND NOSES

Mini twisted salted pretzels, as needed

Red Skittles, as needed

To make the googly eyes, combine the powdered sugar, cornstarch and milk in a small bowl. Whisk the mixture together until it is smooth. Transfer the icing mixture into a piping bag and pipe small white circles onto a piece of parchment paper. Place 1 mini chocolate chip in the middle of each circle. Place the parchment paper in the freezer for 1 to 2 hours.

To make the reindeer cookies, preheat the oven to 350°F (175°C) and line a large baking sheet with parchment paper.

In a large bowl, combine the flour, coconut sugar, baking soda and salt. In a medium bowl, whisk together the coconut oil, peanut butter, milk and vanilla. Pour the coconut oil mixture into the flour mixture and combine with a spatula. Mix in the chocolate chips until combined.

Divide the dough into 12 balls and place them on the prepared baking sheet. Press down on the balls with the bottom of a glass until they are about ¼ inch (6 mm) thick and 2½ inches (6 cm) in diameter. Bake the cookies for 8 to 10 minutes. Remove them from the oven and let them cool for 5 minutes before carefully moving them to a wire rack.

In the meantime, make the frosting. In a small bowl, combine the peanut butter, maple syrup, milk and cacao powder and whisk until the frosting is smooth and thick. Once the cookies have cooled, frost the cookies, then carefully apply the googly eyes, the pretzels as ears and the Skittles as noses before the frosting sets.

MARZIPAN CHALLAH

This beautiful vegan challah is the perfect twist on a holiday classic. The addition of marzipan adds a kick of almond sweetness, which makes it feel like you're eating a Danish pastry. While this recipe might look a bit complicated at first, it's actually fairly easy to make once you get the hang of the braiding, and it's so worth it the moment you bite into a piece of the warm and fluffy deliciousness!

YIELD: 10 servings

CHALLAH

1 tbsp (10 g) instant yeast

¼ cup (48 g) granulated sugar, divided

1 cup plus 3 tbsp (285 ml) warm water, divided

5 tbsp (75 ml) vegetable oil, divided, plus more as needed

1 tbsp (11 g) baking powder

3½ cups (420 g) all-purpose flour, divided

1 tsp salt

MARZIPAN

½ cup (48 g) almond flour

¼ cup (33 g) powdered sugar

1 tsp almond extract

1 tbsp (15 ml) pure maple syrup

To make the challah, place the yeast, a pinch of the ¼ cup (48 g) of granulated sugar and 1 cup (240 ml) of the warm water in a medium bowl and whisk lightly. Let the mixture rest for 3 to 5 minutes, until creamy.

In the meantime, combine the remaining 3 tablespoons (45 ml) of warm water with 2 tablespoons (30 ml) of the oil in a small bowl. Add the baking powder and stir with a spoon until the mixture is fizzy.

In a large bowl, combine 3 cups (360 g) of the all-purpose flour, the remaining ¼ cup (48 g) of granulated sugar and salt and whisk well.

Add the remaining 3 tablespoons (45 ml) of oil to the yeast mixture and combine. Add the baking powder mixture to the oil-yeast mixture. Add the liquid mixture to the all-purpose flour mixture while stirring well with a wooden spoon, then knead with your hands until the dough is smooth, 6 to 8 minutes. If the dough is too sticky, add the remaining ½ cup (60 g) of all-purpose flour a little at a time as you knead. The dough is ready once it doesn't stick to the sides of the bowl anymore.

Lightly grease a large bowl with additional oil. Transfer the dough to the bowl and gently roll it around in the bowl to coat it with the oil. Cover the bowl with a damp kitchen towel and let the dough rise at room temperature for 2 hours or until it has doubled in size.

In the meantime, prepare the marzipan. Combine the almond flour, powdered sugar, almond extract and maple syrup in a food processor and pulse until a sticky mass forms. Wrap the marzipan in parchment paper or plastic wrap and place it in the fridge.

Line a medium baking sheet with parchment paper. Once the dough has risen, place it on a floured surface and knead it for 2 minutes to get rid of any air bubbles.

(continued)

VEGAN EGG WASH

1 tbsp (15 ml) almond milk

1 tbsp (15 ml) pure maple syrup

TOPPING

¼ cup (28 g) slivered blanched almonds

½ tsp ground cinnamon

Dash of powdered sugar (optional)

Divide the dough into 6 equal pieces. Pat and stretch each piece into a long rectangle, making sure they are all the same length, and place about one-sixth of the marzipan in a long strip in the middle of the rectangle. Roll the dough around it and pinch it closed, making a rope that is about 16 inches (40 cm) long. Repeat this process with the remaining 5 pieces of dough.

Arrange the 6 dough ropes next to one another on a work surface. Connect the ends on the top and use your palm to pinch them together so they'll hold well, then tuck them under a bit. For easier braiding, move the A and F ropes up a bit on the work surface so that they form a horizontal line, then move the E and D ropes to the top left a bit and the C and B strands to the top right so there is an empty space in the middle.

Pick up the A rope on the far right and move it all the way over to the left side. Pick up the F rope on the far left and move it all the way to the right side. The F rope should be on top and the A rope below. Then take the F rope from the right side and move it down in the middle between the D and C strands.

As you braid, when you bring the rope down from the right side, you'll replace it with a rope from the left side (and vice versa). Hence, to replace the F rope you just moved, take the second strand from the left (the E rope) and move it all the way to the upper-right side. Then move the D and F ropes to the top-left side to fill the empty space.

Now move the A rope from the upper-left side down into the middle and replace it with the second strand from the right (the B rope). Then move the A and C ropes to the top right to fill the empty space. Now simply continue braiding with this method: Bring the rope down from the right and replace it with the second rope from the left, then bring down the rope from the left and replace it with the second rope from the right until there is no more dough to work with, then pinch the ends together and tuck it under the end.

Transfer the dough to the prepared baking sheet, cover the dough with a damp cloth and let the dough rise for 45 minutes at room temperature.

Preheat the oven to 325°F (160°C).

In the meantime, make the vegan egg wash. In a small bowl, whisk together the milk and maple syrup. Gently brush the wash all over the braided challah and sprinkle the almonds and cinnamon on top. Bake for 23 to 25 minutes, until the bread is golden brown on top. Place the challah on a cooling rack to cool. Dust it with the powdered sugar (if using) prior to serving.

CHOCOLATE MOUSSE CARAMEL DOMES

If you're looking for an incredibly decadent and fancy vegan dessert, this is it. These Chocolate Mousse Caramel Domes have everything I want in an amazing dessert. They're rich yet surprisingly fluffy, absolutely beautiful and just oozing with all that chocolaty goodness. They're not challenging to make; you'll just need specific silicone molds and to plan a bit of time ahead. • **GLUTEN FREE** •

YIELD: 4 servings

CHOCOLATE MOUSSE

½ cup (120 ml) aquafaba (see Quick Tip on page 61)

4.2 oz (118 g) 70% cacao vegan dark chocolate

2 tbsp (30 ml) pure maple syrup

1 tsp coffee extract or pure vanilla extract (optional)

VANILLA SPONGE CAKE

½ cup (120 ml) almond milk

1 tsp apple cider vinegar

1 tbsp (15 ml) melted coconut oil

1 tsp pure vanilla extract

1 cup (96 g) almond flour

¼ cup (25 g) oat flour

1 tbsp (8 g) cornstarch

¼ cup (48 g) coconut sugar

½ tsp baking powder

¼ tsp baking soda

Pinch of salt

To make the chocolate mousse, place the aquafaba in a medium glass bowl. Transfer the bowl to the fridge to chill for 15 minutes.

Place the chocolate in a small glass bowl. Bring a small pot partially filled with water to a simmer over medium-low heat. Place the glass bowl in the pot, making sure the bowl does not actually touch the simmering water. Heat the chocolate until it is melted and smooth, 3 to 4 minutes. Take the pot and bowl off the heat, but leave the bowl sitting over the warm water bath until the chocolate cools to room temperature.

While the chocolate cools, remove the bowl of aquafaba from the fridge and use a stand mixer or electric hand mixer to beat the aquafaba on high until stiff peaks form, 5 to 10 minutes. (Note that aquafaba can't be overbeaten, so it's fine to beat it a bit longer if needed.)

Add the maple syrup and vanilla to the aquafaba and beat for 1 to 2 minutes. The aquafaba is done when you can turn the bowl upside down and the aquafaba stays in place. Pour the cooled melted chocolate into the aquafaba and carefully use a spatula to combine (don't use the mixer or the fluffy aquafaba will deflate).

Spoon the mousse into 4 (2¾-inch [7-cm]) half-circle silicone molds, filling the molds three-quarters full. Place the molds in the freezer for 2 hours.

To make the vanilla sponge cake, preheat the oven to 350°F (175°C). Line an 8 x 8–inch (20 x 20–cm) baking pan with parchment paper.

In a medium bowl, combine the milk and vinegar. Set it aside to let the milk curdle for 5 minutes to achieve vegan buttermilk. Add the oil and vanilla and combine.

In a large bowl, whisk together the almond flour, oat flour, cornstarch, sugar, baking powder, baking soda and salt. Pour the milk mixture into the flour mixture and stir just enough to form a batter (don't overmix). Pour the batter into the prepared baking pan and bake for 10 minutes, until a toothpick inserted into the center comes out clean. Remove the cake from the oven and let it cool, then use a glass or cookie cutter to cut out 4 circles the size of the silicone molds.

(continued)

CARAMEL

½ cup (90 g) almond butter

4 tbsp (60 ml) pure maple syrup

1 tsp pure vanilla extract

CHOCOLATE GANACHE

3.5 oz (98 g) 70% cacao vegan dark chocolate

½ cup (120 ml) almond milk

GARNISHES

Finely chopped nuts (optional)

Edible gold glitter (optional)

To make the caramel, whisk together the almond butter, maple syrup and vanilla in a small bowl. Once the chocolate mousse has set, spoon 1 to 2 tablespoons (15 to 30 ml) of the caramel on top of each serving of chocolate mousse. Place the sponge cake circles on top and press down slightly. Place the molds in the freezer for 2 hours, until the caramel is completely firm.

Once the caramel is firm, prepare the chocolate ganache. Place the chocolate in a small glass bowl. Bring a small pot partially filled with water to a simmer over medium-low heat. Place the glass bowl in the pot, making sure the bowl does not actually touch the simmering water. Heat the chocolate until it is melted and smooth, 3 to 4 minutes.

Meanwhile, heat the milk in a small saucepan over medium heat. Remove the milk from the heat just before it begins boiling and add it to the melted chocolate. Whisk until the two are fully combined and smooth.

Remove the mousse domes from the freezer and place them on a wire rack. Place a parchment paper–lined baking sheet under the rack to catch the chocolate. Immediately pour the chocolate ganache over the domes until they are completely coated. Place the domes in the fridge for 5 minutes, then place them on serving plates and return them to the fridge for 2 hours before serving. Garnish the domes with the nuts and glitter (if desired).

QUICK TIP: If you're unfamiliar with aquafaba, it's simply the strained liquid from canned unsalted chickpeas.

CINNAMON ICE CREAM

Waking up on Christmas morning to the smell of my mum's homemade cinnamon ice cream is one of my favorite memories. I'd wait all day long just to eat a few scoops of this creamy and heavenly spiced treat. Of course, I had to create a vegan version of my favorite Christmas dessert and got myself an ice cream machine just for the occasion! Get ready to have your taste buds blown away by this amazingly rich and decadent treat. • **GLUTEN FREE** •

YIELD: 6 servings

2 (14-oz [420-ml]) cans full-fat coconut cream

3 tbsp (36 g) coconut sugar

⅓ cup (80 ml) pure maple syrup

1 tsp pure vanilla extract

1 tbsp (8 g) ground cinnamon

Pinch of salt

Combine the cream and sugar in a medium saucepan over medium heat. Bring the mixture to a boil and whisk for 1 to 2 minutes. Remove the saucepan from the heat and stir in the maple syrup, vanilla, cinnamon and salt.

Transfer the mixture to a large glass bowl and refrigerate until the mixture has cooled. Once the mixture is chilled, pour it into the bowl of an ice cream machine and mix according to the manufacturer's instructions. (This will take anywhere from 30 to 45 minutes.)

When the ice cream machine stops, transfer the ice cream to a freezer-safe container. At this point, you can either serve it as soft-serve ice cream or you can freeze it for harder ice cream. Thaw hardened ice cream for 10 minutes before serving.

Classic THANKSGIVING EATS

As one of the most eagerly celebrated holidays, Thanksgiving is truly special—and a vegan Thanksgiving can be even more so! It's a time to come together, give thanks and spread kindness to animals as well as to your loved ones. Long gone are the days when a turkey had to be the centerpiece of the Thanksgiving feast. Instead, dig into delicious nut roasts, stuffed pumpkins and creamy casseroles, as well as flavorful vegan classics such as the Mac 'n' Cheese Bake (page 76), Miso-Tofu Meatballs (page 80), Sourdough Bread Stuffing (page 88), Fluffy Cornbread (page 92) and Lemon-Rosemary Roasted Potatoes (page 91).

It wouldn't be a real Thanksgiving feast without a bunch of decadent desserts, though, so make sure to leave some space for Layered No-Bake Pumpkin Cheesecake (page 95), Chocolate Mousse Pie (page 109), Nutty Fudge Brownies (page 106) and Spiced Pumpkin Cream Roll (page 96)!

STUFFED BUTTERNUT SQUASH

This stunning vegetable entrée will most likely steal the show at your plant-based Thanksgiving! The juicy butternut squash, filled with a flavorful nut paste and layered zucchini, replaces the usual meaty suspects. And the garlic butter gives you a smooth finish to the perfect holiday dish. • **GLUTEN FREE** •

YIELD: 6 to 8 servings

STUFFED BUTTERNUT SQUASH

½ cup (70 g) almonds

½ cup (60 g) pecans

1 cup (120 g) dried breadcrumbs

1 medium butternut squash

1 small zucchini

1 medium red onion, diced

2 cloves garlic, minced

1 large portobello mushroom, finely chopped

1 tbsp (15 ml) olive oil

2 tbsp (10 g) nutritional yeast

2 tbsp (30 ml) soy sauce or tamari

½ tsp salt

¼ tsp black pepper

¼ tsp red pepper flakes

¼ cup (10 g) fresh parsley, finely chopped

To make the stuffed butternut squash, preheat the oven to 350°F (175°C) and line a large baking sheet with parchment paper.

Place the almonds and pecans on the prepared baking sheet and toast them in the oven for 5 to 10 minutes. Remove the nuts from the oven and let them cool down. Combine the nuts and breadcrumbs in a high-speed blender or food processor. Pulse a few times until the ingredients are crumbly.

Cut the butternut squash and the zucchini lengthwise. Use a melon baller to remove the squash's seeds. Scoop out the flesh of the zucchini halves as well, leaving a ¾-inch (19-mm)-wide path down the middle of each half, and set the zucchini flesh aside. Repeat this step with the butternut squash, leaving a ½-inch (13-mm) border on all sides—there is no need to reserve the squash flesh. Make sure the zucchini halves fit into the butternut squash halves. Using a fork, pierce the insides of the squash and zucchini halves.

Combine the reserved zucchini flesh, onion, garlic and mushroom in a food processor and process until a thick paste forms.

Heat the oil in a medium skillet over medium heat. Add the zucchini mixture. Cook for 3 to 5 minutes, until the paste is golden brown. Transfer the paste to the food processor and add the nut mixture, nutritional yeast, soy sauce, salt, black pepper and red pepper flakes. Process until the paste is thick, scraping down the sides as needed. Transfer the paste to a medium bowl and mix in the parsley.

Place the squash halves, cut-sides up, on the prepared baking sheet. Use the back of a spoon to press 3 to 4 tablespoons (45 to 60 g) of the vegetable-nut paste into each half, until the sides and bottom are fully coated. Nestle the zucchini halves, cut-sides up, into the squash halves and fill them with the paste. Make sure to fill any gaps between the zucchini and squash with any remaining paste, then top the one squash half with the other.

(continued)

GARLIC BUTTER

3 tbsp (42 g) vegan butter

2 cloves garlic, minced

Pinch of salt

1 tsp pure maple syrup

2 tbsp (6 g) fresh parsley, finely chopped

Cut 2 pieces of kitchen twine and tie them tightly around the butternut squash halves to seal them. Wrap the squash in aluminum foil or parchment paper and secure it in the center of the baking sheet by placing small oven-safe bowls or pans on the sides to keep it from moving.

Bake the squash until it is tender to the touch, 1½ to 2 hours. Take it out of the oven and let it rest while you prepare the garlic butter.

To make the garlic butter, melt the butter in a small saucepan over medium heat. Add the garlic, salt, maple syrup and parsley and fry for 1 minute.

When ready to serve, slice the butternut squash and drizzle a spoonful of the garlic butter on top.

GLUTEN-FREE SUBSTITUTE: Instead of using breadcrumbs, you can use unsalted gluten-free pretzels. Simply grind them into fine crumbs in a food processor or coffee grinder.

BALSAMIC-ROASTED BEETROOT SALAD WITH ALMOND FETA

If you're a beet lover like I am and are trying to switch up the usual Thanksgiving sides, you're going to love this salad! This colorful and healthy option will surely brighten up any Thanksgiving spread. Roasting the beets brings out their natural sweetness and the combination of a tangy almond feta with a balsamic-maple vinaigrette is heavenly. You can make the almond feta days ahead and simply store it in the fridge; serve it as a spread on its own or use it for salads such as this one. • GLUTEN FREE •

YIELD: 4 SERVINGS

ALMOND FETA

1 cup (140 g) raw almonds, blanched

2 tbsp (30 ml) fresh lemon juice

1 tbsp (15 ml) apple cider vinegar

1 to 2 cloves garlic

2 tbsp (10 g) nutritional yeast

1 tbsp (15 ml) olive oil

¼ cup (60 ml) water

½ tsp salt

Dash of black pepper

SALAD

6 medium beets, trimmed, peeled and diced

1 tbsp (15 ml) olive oil

Pinch of salt, plus more as needed

4 oz (112 g) baby arugula

⅓ cup (45 g) roasted pine nuts

Black pepper, to taste (optional)

To make the almond feta, soak the blanched almonds in water for 4 to 6 hours. Drain and rinse them, then transfer them to a high-speed blender. Add the lemon juice, apple cider vinegar, garlic, nutritional yeast, oil, water, salt and black pepper and blend on low at first; then blend on high until you get a rather smooth mixture (use your tamper tool to mash the mixture down as needed).

Place a sieve over a medium bowl and place a four-layered piece of cheesecloth inside the sieve. Scoop the almond mixture into the cheesecloth, then bring all four corners together so you have the almond mixture sealed in a ball. Squeeze out any extra liquid and tighten the ball with an elastic band. Place the cheeseball in the fridge for 12 hours.

Preheat the oven to 350°F (175°C) and line a small baking sheet with parchment paper.

Carefully unwrap the feta, place it on the prepared baking sheet and bake for 30 minutes, until the top is golden brown and cracking. Remove it from the baking sheet and let it cool.

To make the salad, increase the oven temperature to 400°F (200°C).

Place the beets on the same baking sheet. Toss them with the oil and salt. Roast for 45 to 50 minutes, until the beets are tender.

(continued)

BALSAMIC-MAPLE VINAIGRETTE

2 tbsp (30 ml) olive oil

2 tbsp (30 ml) balsamic vinegar

2 tbsp (30 ml) pure maple syrup

1 tsp Dijon mustard

Meanwhile, make the balsamic-maple vinaigrette. Whisk together the oil, balsamic vinegar, maple syrup and mustard in a small bowl.

Place the arugula in a serving bowl, add the beets and pine nuts and toss the salad with the desired amount of vinaigrette. Place small pieces of the almond feta on top, drizzle the salad with any remaining vinaigrette and season the salad with salt and black pepper (if desired) before serving.

QUICK TIP: If you don't have enough time to soak your nuts but still want to achieve that smooth consistency when blending, simply boil your nuts in a pot of water for 10 to 15 minutes and drain them thoroughly before placing them in your blender.

BARLEY-NUT ROAST WITH CRANBERRY SAUCE

A good vegan nut roast is a beautiful centerpiece at any plant-based Thanksgiving. With a combination of sweet and savory, this mouthwatering barley-nut roast hits all the right spots! • **GLUTEN FREE** •

YIELD: 8 to 10 servings

BARLEY-NUT ROAST

2 tbsp (30 ml) olive oil, divided

1 medium red onion, finely chopped

2 cups (150 g) roughly chopped chestnut or cremini mushrooms

2 cloves garlic, minced

1 tbsp (3 g) finely chopped fresh rosemary

¾ cup (140 g) pearl barley

3 cups (720 ml) vegetable broth

¾ cup (90 g) unsalted pistachios, plus more as needed

1 cup (120 g) pecans, plus more as needed

2 tbsp (10 g) quick oats

Zest of 1 lemon

2 tbsp (16 g) tapioca flour

1 tsp salt

Black pepper, to taste

CRANBERRY SAUCE

1 tsp tapioca flour

¼ cup (60 ml) water, divided

¼ cup (30 g) dried cranberries, plus more as needed

1 tbsp (15 ml) pure maple syrup

1 tsp fresh lemon juice

Heat 1 tablespoon (15 ml) of the oil in a large saucepan over medium heat. Add the onion and cook for 5 minutes, until it is golden brown. Add the mushrooms and cook for 5 minutes. Add the garlic and rosemary and cook for 2 minutes. Increase the heat to medium-high and add the barley.

Cook the mixture, stirring, for 1 minute, then add the broth, 1 cup (240 ml) at a time, until each addition has been completely absorbed (this process will take about 15 minutes). Stir the mixture continuously, as this will make it creamy. Once all the liquid is absorbed, transfer the mixture to a large bowl and allow it to cool.

Preheat the oven to 350°F (175°C). Line an 8-inch (20-cm) loaf pan with parchment paper or grease it with oil.

Combine the pistachios, pecans and oats in a food processor and pulse 1 to 3 times, until the ingredients are crumbly but still coarse. Add the nut mixture to the barley mixture. Add the lemon zest, tapioca flour, salt and black pepper and adjust the seasonings to your liking. Combine everything until the mixture is creamy.

Transfer the barley-nut mixture to the prepared loaf pan. Use a spoon to press the loaf down evenly, then wrap the loaf pan in aluminum foil and bake the roast in the oven for 60 minutes. Once it is golden brown on top, remove it from the oven and let it cool for 10 minutes before removing it from the loaf pan and placing it on a serving platter.

While the roast cools, prepare the cranberry sauce. Dissolve the tapioca flour in 1 teaspoon of the water to create a slurry. Set aside. Place the cranberries, maple syrup, lemon juice and remaining water in a small saucepan over medium-high heat and cook for 5 minutes, until the cranberries are soft. Add the tapioca slurry, stirring constantly, until the sauce has thickened slightly. Spoon the cranberry sauce onto the roast and serve.

ROASTED ACORN SQUASH WITH QUINOA STUFFING

This roasted and stuffed acorn squash is the perfect holiday dish! Packed with flavorful
and fragrant quinoa stuffing, this cozy dish is sure to impress, leaving you satisfied on a sweet but
hearty note. • GLUTEN FREE •

YIELD: 4 servings

ACORN SQUASH

4 medium acorn squash

GLAZE

1 tsp olive oil

1 tbsp (15 ml) pure maple syrup

STUFFING

½ cup (85 g) uncooked quinoa

1 cup (240 ml) vegetable broth

2 tbsp (30 ml) olive oil

1 medium red onion, diced

½ medium red apple, diced

⅓ cup (40 g) pecans, finely chopped

1 tbsp (15 ml) pure maple syrup

4 cremini or white button
mushrooms, diced

1 tbsp (15 ml) soy sauce

½ tsp ground cinnamon

1 tbsp (3 g) fresh thyme leaves

Pinch of salt

⅓ cup (65 g) fresh pomegranate
seeds (see Quick Tip)

To prepare the acorn squash, preheat the oven to 350°F (175°C) and line a
medium baking sheet with parchment paper. Cut off the top of each acorn
squash as well as a thin slice from the bottom so it will stand on its own.
Remove the seeds and some of the squash flesh to make a bowl, being
careful not to scoop out too much on the bottom side.

To make the glaze, combine the oil and maple syrup in a small bowl, then
brush each squash evenly with the glaze. Place the squash on the prepared
baking sheet and roast for 30 minutes.

Meanwhile, make the stuffing. Cook the quinoa in the broth according to
the quinoa package's instructions. In the meantime, heat the oil in a large
nonstick skillet over medium heat. Add the onion, apple, pecans and maple
syrup and cook for 3 to 4 minutes, until the apple is soft and the onion is
golden brown. Add the mushrooms, soy sauce, cinnamon, thyme and salt
and cook for 5 to 10 minutes. Once the quinoa is done, add it to the pan
and cook for 3 to 5 minutes, until the flavors have combined.

Remove the squash from the oven. Fill each squash with the quinoa stuffing,
then return the squash to the oven and roast for 10 minutes.

Remove the squash from the oven, divide the pomegranate seeds among
them and serve warm.

QUICK TIP: When buying whole pomegranates, there's a very easy trick to
take out the seeds without making a mess. Simply slice the pomegranate into
4 pieces, place them in a big bowl with water and separate the seeds from
the skin under water. The seeds will sink to the bottom while the skin will float
on top!

GLUTEN-FREE SUBSTITUTE: To make this recipe gluten free, follow the
note on page 20 (soy sauce).

MAC 'N' CHEESE BAKE

There's nothing that better symbolizes comforting, feel-good food than a heaping plate of this Mac 'n' Cheese Bake. It's cheesy, uber creamy and the perfect vegan version of a beloved holiday classic. It's perfected with a crispy baked Parmesan layer, and it's ready to be served in only 30 minutes! • **GLUTEN FREE** •

YIELD: 6 servings

MAC 'N' CHEESE

14 oz (400 g) brown rice elbow pasta (or any variety)

Olive oil, as needed

1 medium russet potato, peeled and quartered

1 medium carrot, peeled and chopped into ½-inch (13-mm) pieces

¾ cup (113 g) raw cashews

1 tbsp (14 g) vegan butter or 1 tbsp (15 ml) olive oil

1 small onion, diced

2 cloves garlic, minced

1 cup (240 ml) water

¼ cup (60 ml) almond or soy milk

1 tbsp (15 ml) fresh lemon juice

¼ cup (20 g) nutritional yeast

½ tsp Dijon mustard

¼ tsp salt

⅛ tsp black pepper

Finely chopped fresh parsley, as needed

VEGAN PARMESAN

½ cup (70 g) blanched almonds

2 tbsp (10 g) nutritional yeast

1 tsp salt

1 tsp garlic powder

1 tsp onion powder

To make the mac 'n' cheese, preheat the oven to 350°F (175°C) and grease a 7 x 10–inch (18 x 25–cm) baking dish. Bring a large pot of water to a boil over high heat. Add the pasta and cook according to the package's instructions, until it is al dente. Drain the pasta and toss it with a drizzle of the oil to prevent it from sticking, then transfer it back to the pot.

Bring a medium pot of water to a boil over high heat. Add the potato, carrot and cashews, reduce the heat to medium and cook for 10 to 12 minutes, until the vegetables are soft. Drain the pot and transfer the potato, carrot and cashews to a high-speed blender.

Heat the butter in a small skillet over medium heat. Add the onion and garlic and cook for 3 to 4 minutes, until they are golden brown. Transfer the onion and garlic to the blender. Add the water, milk, lemon juice, nutritional yeast, mustard, salt and black pepper to the blender. Blend for 1 to 2 minutes, until the sauce is completely smooth. Pour the sauce over the cooked pasta and combine until covered completely.

To make the vegan Parmesan, combine the almonds, nutritional yeast, salt, garlic powder and onion powder in a blender and pulse a few seconds, until the mixture is crumbly.

Pour the pasta into the prepared baking dish and add a layer of vegan Parmesan on top. Bake for 8 to 10 minutes, until the mac 'n' cheese is crispy on top. Serve with the parsley on top.

MUSHROOM-CHESTNUT TART

This mushroom-chestnut tart is simply delicious—the festive flavors and creamy filling make this vegan tart a great alternative to a roast for Thanksgiving or Christmas. If you can't find wild mushrooms, simply double the others. This dish is perfect to make a day ahead of time, too.

YIELD: 8 servings

CRUST

1⅓ cups (160 g) all-purpose flour

1 tsp tapioca flour

Pinch of salt

½ cup (113 g) vegan butter, softened

1 tbsp (15 ml) cold water

CHEESY SAUCE

1 cup (150 g) raw cashews, soaked 6 to 8 hours (or overnight) and drained

1 cup (240 ml) soy milk

1 cup (225 g) pumpkin puree

¼ cup (20 g) nutritional yeast

1 tbsp (15 ml) fresh lemon juice

½ tsp salt

⅛ tsp black pepper

½ tsp paprika

2 tbsp (16 g) tapioca flour

FILLING

2 tbsp (30 ml) olive oil

1 large onion, finely chopped

3 cloves garlic, minced

2 cups (150 g) roughly chopped chanterelle mushrooms

2 cups (150 g) thinly sliced chestnut or cremini mushrooms

¼ cup (60 ml) soy sauce

2 cups (280 g) cooked chestnuts

⅓ cup (13 g) fresh parsley, plus more as needed, roughly chopped

To make the crust, sift the all-purpose flour, tapioca flour and salt into a large bowl. Add the butter and use a hand mixer fitted with kneading hooks to combine the mixture until it's crumbly, about 2 minutes. Add the water and continue mixing until the mixture begins to pull together to form a dough, about 3 minutes. Using your hands, form a ball, knead the ball lightly for 1 minute, wrap it in parchment paper and place it in the fridge for 30 minutes.

To make the cheesy sauce, combine the drained cashews, milk, pumpkin puree, nutritional yeast, lemon juice, salt, black pepper, paprika and tapioca flour in a high-speed blender and blend for 1 to 2 minutes, until the sauce is smooth.

To make the filling, heat the oil in a large saucepan over medium heat. Add the onion and garlic and fry for 3 to 4 minutes, until they are golden brown. Add the chanterelle mushrooms, chestnut mushrooms and soy sauce and cook for 5 to 8 minutes. Add the chestnuts and parsley and cook for 5 minutes, then set the filling aside. Pour the cheesy sauce into the saucepan and use a spoon to combine the filling and sauce.

Preheat the oven to 350°F (175°C). Grease a 10½-inch (26-cm)-deep tart tin. On a floured work surface, roll out the dough into a circle slightly larger than the tart tin. Carefully roll the pastry over the rolling pin and transfer it to the tart tin. Press the pastry into the sides of the tin and trim the edges.

Carefully spoon the cheesy filling into the pastry and spread it out evenly. Bake the tart for 35 to 40 minutes, until the pastry is crisp. Remove the tart from the oven, set it aside and let it cool slightly. Sprinkle extra parsley on top and serve.

MISO-TOFU MEATBALLS

Giving a vegan twist to the traditional Thanksgiving turkey meatballs, these little tofu bombs are an absolute winner! They're perfectly crisp on the outside and extremely tender and flavorful on the inside, thanks to the Asian-inspired addition of miso. Serve them as an appetizer on their own or turn these tofu meatballs into a meal by serving them with spaghetti or mashed potatoes and some gravy. • GLUTEN FREE •

YIELD: 3 to 4 servings

SPAGHETTI

14 oz (400 g) spaghetti or any gluten-free pasta

3 cups (720 ml) marinara sauce

¼ cup (10 g) fresh basil leaves

¼ cup (45 g) Vegan Parmesan (page 76)

TOFU MEATBALLS

1 tbsp (7 g) ground flaxseed

3 tbsp (45 ml) water

2 tbsp (30 ml) olive oil, divided

1 medium white onion, diced

2 cloves garlic, minced

⅓ cup (40 g) walnuts

¼ cup (20 g) nutritional yeast

7 oz (196 g) firm tofu

1 tsp miso paste (any variety)

¼ cup (10 g) fresh parsley

1 tbsp (3 g) Italian seasoning

½ tsp salt

¼ tsp black pepper

To make the spaghetti, bring a medium pot of water to a boil over high heat. Cook the spaghetti according to the package's instructions, until al dente, then drain and immediately transfer it back to the pot. Toss the spaghetti with the marinara sauce to prevent sticking and cover the pot.

To make the tofu meatballs, prepare a flax egg by combining the flaxseed with the water in a small bowl. Set the mixture aside for 3 to 5 minutes.

Preheat the oven to 400°F (200°C) and line a large baking sheet with parchment paper.

In a medium skillet over medium-high heat, heat 1 tablespoon (15 ml) of the oil and fry the onion and garlic for 3 to 4 minutes, until they are golden brown.

In a food processor, combine the walnuts and nutritional yeast and pulse a few times until the mixture is crumbly. Crumble the tofu into a few large pieces with your hands and add them to the food processor. Add the miso, parsley, Italian seasoning, salt and black pepper. Pulse a few times and scrape down the sides until a thick, paste-like mixture forms. Transfer the mixture to a medium bowl and add the onion, garlic and flax egg. Use a spoon or your hands to combine the ingredients. Form small balls with the mixture. Place them on the prepared baking sheet and spray or brush them with the remaining 1 tablespoon (15 ml) of oil. Bake the meatballs for 5 minutes, then flip them over and bake for another 5 minutes, until they are slightly crisp and browned.

Reheat the spaghetti if necessary and serve the meatballs on top with the basil and a sprinkle of the Vegan Parmesan.

QUICK TIP: You can make a vegan egg using either ground flax or chia seeds. Simply grind the seeds in a coffee grinder or high-speed blender or buy them already ground. The ratio is 1 tablespoon (7 g) of ground seeds whisked together with 3 tablespoons (45 ml) of water. After 5 to 8 minutes, the mixture will take on an egg-like, stretchy consistency.

SWEET POTATO AND CAULIFLOWER CASSEROLE

Hearty casseroles always remind me of my childhood and this one is no exception. Creamy and loaded with veggies, this comforting dish is not only good for you but will also satisfy your soul. • **GLUTEN FREE** •

YIELD: 4 to 6 servings

CHEESE SAUCE

1 cup (150 g) raw cashews, soaked for 6 to 8 hours (or overnight)

1½ cups (360 ml) almond or soy milk

½ tsp ground turmeric

¼ cup (20 g) nutritional yeast

¼ tsp salt

⅛ tsp black pepper

VEGGIES

2 medium sweet potatoes, peeled and diced

1 small head cauliflower, chopped into small florets

1 medium red onion, thinly sliced

2 tbsp (6 g) finely chopped fresh parsley, plus more as needed

MARINADE

½ cup (120 g) tahini or almond butter

1 tsp garlic powder

1 tsp pure maple syrup

1 tbsp (16 g) Dijon mustard

1 tbsp (15 ml) apple cider vinegar

⅓ cup (80 ml) water

¼ tsp salt

⅛ tsp black pepper

To make the cheese sauce, drain the cashews and place them in a blender. Add the milk, turmeric, nutritional yeast, salt and black pepper and blend until the sauce is smooth.

To make the veggies, preheat the oven to 400°F (200°C) and grease a 7 x 10–inch (18 x 25–cm) baking dish.

While the oven is preheating, combine the sweet potatoes, cauliflower, onion and parsley in a large bowl.

To make the marinade, whisk together the tahini, garlic powder, maple syrup, mustard, vinegar, water, salt and black pepper in a medium bowl until the marinade is smooth. Pour the marinade over the veggies and use your hands or a large spoon to coat them all.

Transfer the veggies to the prepared baking dish and spread them out evenly. Pour the cheese sauce on top and make sure all the veggies are covered. Bake, covered, for 45 minutes. Uncover the casserole and bake for another 30 minutes, until the veggies are soft and the top is golden brown. Let the casserole cool slightly and serve with additional parsley.

SWEET POTATO GNOCCHI IN SAGE BUTTER

Is there anything better than enjoying delicious gnocchi that are crispy on the outside and soft on the inside? For a holiday twist, these gnocchi are made with sweet potatoes, but they could also be easily made with any leftover pumpkin—they are super easy to make and incredibly flavorful!

YIELD: 7 to 8 servings

ALMOND-CASHEW PARMESAN

¼ cup (35 g) raw almonds

¼ cup (38 g) raw cashews

1 tbsp (7 g) dried breadcrumbs (optional)

¼ cup (20 g) nutritional yeast

½ tsp salt

SWEET POTATO GNOCCHI

2½ lb (1.1 kg) sweet potatoes

4½ to 5 cups (520 to 575 g) spelt flour

2 tbsp (16 g) tapioca flour

½ tsp salt

Dash of black pepper

Olive oil, as needed

SAGE BUTTER

6 tbsp (84 g) vegan butter

1 small white onion, diced

2 cloves garlic, minced

6 tbsp (18 g) fresh sage, finely chopped

Salt and black pepper, to taste

To make the almond-cashew Parmesan, combine all the Parmesan ingredients in a food processor or high-speed blender. Pulse until the mixture is crumbly. Set it aside.

To make the sweet potato gnocchi, preheat the oven to 350°F (175°C) and line a medium baking sheet with parchment paper. Pierce the sweet potatoes with a fork. Place them on the prepared baking sheet and bake for 30 to 40 minutes, until soft. Let the sweet potatoes cool until they can be handled safely. Scoop the sweet potato flesh into a large bowl, discarding the potato skins. Mash the sweet potato flesh with a fork into a smooth puree. Add the spelt flour, tapioca flour, salt and black pepper and very gently knead the mixture into a dough (don't over-knead it or it will get tough).

Place the dough on a floured work surface and roll it into 8 to 10 separate ropes. Cut each rope into 1-inch (2.5-cm)-thick segments. Use a fork to roll over each gnocchi to achieve that authentic gnocchi design and place the gnocchi aside. Bring a large pot of water to a boil over high heat. Reduce the heat to medium, add the gnocchi in batches and cook for 5 minutes, until they rise to the top of the water. Drain the gnocchi and gently toss them with a little drizzle of oil to prevent sticking.

To make the sage butter, heat the butter in a large skillet over medium heat. Add the onion and fry for 1 to 2 minutes, until it is golden brown. Add the garlic, sage and gnocchi and cook for 1 to 2 minutes, until the gnocchi are golden brown and crispy on the outside. Season with the salt and pepper, then serve immediately with a sprinkle of the almond-cashew Parmesan on top.

GLUTEN-FREE SUBSTITUTE FOR FLOUR: When replacing spelt flour in gnocchi, use a gluten-free all-purpose flour blend. You'll usually need a bit extra: 1 to 2 tablespoons (6 to 12 g) per 1 cup (90 g) of flour.

GLUTEN-FREE SUBSTITUTE: For a tip on breadcrumbs, see page 68.

CAULIFLOWER-POTATO MASH

A large bowl of this buttery, fluffy, comforting cauliflower-potato mash is the ultimate Thanksgiving side dish—at least in my opinion! Mashed potatoes are one of the easiest classics to veganize, as the use of almond or soy milk and vegan butter will give you almost the same results as dairy products. If you're not a big fan of cauliflower, simply add 2 to 3 more potatoes and get your spoon ready to dig into this luxurious bowl of goodness. • **GLUTEN FREE** •

....

YIELD: 4 servings

½ small head cauliflower, cut into florets

5 to 6 medium Yukon gold potatoes, peeled and diced

3 tbsp (42 g) vegan butter, divided

2 shallots, diced

2 cloves garlic, minced

2 tbsp (30 ml) almond or soy milk

2 tbsp (10 g) nutritional yeast

1 tsp salt

¼ tsp ground nutmeg

⅛ tsp black pepper

Place the cauliflower and potatoes in a large pot and cover them with water. Bring the water to a boil, reduce the heat to medium and cook for 25 to 30 minutes, until the vegetables are very tender. Drain the cauliflower and potatoes and place them back in the hot pot off the heat to absorb any additional water.

Heat 1 tablespoon (14 g) of the butter in a small saucepan over high heat. Add the shallots and garlic and cook for 3 to 4 minutes, until they are golden brown. Place the cauliflower, potatoes, shallots and garlic in a large bowl and mash them together using either a potato masher or a hand mixer until they are fluffy (be careful not to overmix or the mash will become gluey). Add the remaining 2 tablespoons (28 g) of butter, milk, nutritional yeast, salt, nutmeg and black pepper and stir to combine. Taste and adjust the seasonings as needed and serve.

SOURDOUGH BREAD STUFFING

This classic Thanksgiving side dish is incredibly easy to make yet full of vegan-friendly flavor. It has a subtle zing in every bite and is very hearty, satisfying and oh so filling! Stuffing is such a popular dish that it's usually the first one to run out at the holiday table, so make sure to pile on enough of this "just like grandma used to make" stuffing!

YIELD: 6 to 8 servings

8 cups (350 g) sourdough bread, cubed (or any other bread)

3 tbsp (42 g) vegan butter or 3 tbsp (45 ml) olive oil

1 medium white onion, roughly chopped

2 to 3 medium ribs celery, thinly sliced

4 cloves garlic, minced

1 tbsp (3 g) finely chopped fresh sage

1 tbsp (3 g) finely chopped fresh thyme

2 cups (150 g) thinly sliced cremini mushrooms

2 to 3 cups (480 to 720 ml) vegetable broth

Salt and black pepper, to taste

Preheat the oven to 350°F (175°C) and line a large baking sheet with parchment paper. Grease a 7 x 10–inch (18 x 25–cm) baking dish.

Spread the bread cubes out evenly on the prepared baking sheet. Toast the bread in the oven for 10 to 15 minutes, flipping it halfway (being careful not to let it burn). Increase the oven temperature to 375°F (190°C) and place the toasted bread cubes in a large bowl.

Heat the butter in a large saucepan over medium heat. Add the onion and celery and sauté until they are translucent, 4 to 5 minutes. Add the garlic, sage and thyme and sauté for 2 minutes. Add the mushrooms and a splash of the broth and cook for 5 to 7 minutes, until the mushrooms are soft and their moisture has evaporated somewhat. Add the mixture to the bread cubes and combine with a spoon.

Transfer the bread mixture to the prepared baking dish. Pour the remaining broth over the bread mixture and carefully combine, until the bread is just saturated—not too wet and not dry. Season with the salt and black pepper and bake for 30 minutes, until the top of the stuffing is crunchy. Let the stuffing cool slightly and serve.

LEMON-ROSEMARY ROASTED POTATOES

These roasted potatoes are on my holiday most-wanted list and frequently raved about by my friends and family. I have fond memories of digging into several trays of these whenever my mum made them during Thanksgiving. While my family has come to love several variations of roasted potatoes, these are the ones that always stood out for me. They are perfectly paired with any main dish and so full of tangy lemon flavor, you just have to love them! • **GLUTEN FREE** •

YIELD: 5 to 6 servings

10 medium Yukon gold or russet potatoes, peeled and quartered

¼ cup (60 ml) olive oil

1 tbsp (8 g) garlic powder

Salt and black pepper, to taste

2 to 3 tbsp (6 to 9 g) finely chopped fresh rosemary

1 tbsp (15 ml) fresh lemon juice

1 lemon, sliced and quartered

Bring a large pot of water to a boil over high heat. Add the potatoes, reduce the heat to medium and parboil the potatoes for 7 to 8 minutes. Drain the potatoes and let them dry for 2 minutes.

Preheat the oven to 400°F (200°C) and line a large baking sheet with parchment paper.

In a large bowl, combine the oil, garlic powder, salt, black pepper, rosemary, lemon juice and lemon slices. Add the potatoes and carefully toss until they are coated in the oil. Spread out the potatoes on the prepared baking sheet and roast for 35 to 40 minutes, turning halfway through the cooking time, until they are golden brown.

FLUFFY CORNBREAD

Whether you have them as a side with chili or topped with vegan butter and jam, these fluffy vegan squares shouldn't be missing from your Thanksgiving table! Slightly sweetened with applesauce, this cornbread is on the healthier side so you can indulge in more than just one piece.

YIELD: 5 to 6 servings

2 tbsp (14 g) ground flaxseed

6 tbsp (90 ml) water

1 cup (240 ml) soy milk

1 tbsp (15 ml) apple cider vinegar

3 tbsp (42 g) vegan butter, melted, or 3 tbsp (45 ml) olive oil

¼ cup (60 g) unsweetened applesauce

¼ cup (56 g) pumpkin puree

¼ cup (60 ml) pure maple syrup

1 cup (170 g) cornmeal

1 cup (120 g) all-purpose flour

1 tsp baking powder

½ tsp baking soda (use 1 tsp if using gluten-free flour)

Pinch of turmeric (optional)

½ tsp salt

½ cup (85 g) corn kernels (optional)

Preheat the oven to 350°F (175°C) and line an 8 x 8–inch (20 x 20–cm) baking pan with parchment paper.

Make the flax eggs by combining the flaxseed with the water in a small bowl. Set the mixture aside and let it thicken.

In a medium bowl, combine the milk with the vinegar and let the milk curdle for 5 minutes to achieve vegan buttermilk. Add the butter, applesauce, pumpkin puree, flax eggs and maple syrup and stir to combine.

In a large bowl, combine the cornmeal, flour, baking powder, baking soda, turmeric and salt and whisk together. Pour the milk mixture into the cornmeal mixture and use a spatula to carefully combine. Mix in the corn kernels (if using) and pour the batter into the baking pan, spreading it out evenly. Bake the cornbread for 20 to 25 minutes and let it cool for at least 10 minutes before slicing.

GLUTEN-FREE SUBSTITUTE: When replacing all-purpose flour in baked goods, either use a gluten-free all-purpose flour blend (Bob's Red Mill has a great one) or use gluten-free oat flour. You'll usually need a bit extra: 1 to 2 tablespoons (6 to 12 g) per 1 cup (90 g) of flour.

LAYERED NO-BAKE PUMPKIN CHEESECAKE

A good vegan cheesecake should be the centerpiece of any celebration! Instead of going with the classic baked version, why not try this deliciously creamy no-bake cheesecake? The addition of pumpkin and delicious fall spices make this the ideal treat to impress. • GLUTEN FREE •

YIELD: 8 SERVINGS

CRUST

¾ cup (105 g) raw almonds

¾ cup (56 g) unsweetened shredded coconut

10 Medjool dates, pitted

½ tsp ground cinnamon

Pinch of salt

1 tbsp (15 ml) almond milk

CREAM LAYER

¾ cup (113 g) raw cashews, soaked for 6 to 8 hours (or overnight) and drained

½ cup (113 g) solid chilled coconut cream

3 tbsp (45 ml) melted coconut oil

2 tbsp (30 ml) pure maple syrup

½ tsp pumpkin pie spice

2 tbsp (30 ml) fresh lemon juice

PUMPKIN LAYER

¾ cup (113 g) raw cashews, soaked 6 to 8 hours (or overnight) and drained

¼ cup (56 g) solid chilled coconut cream

1 cup (225 g) pumpkin puree

3 tbsp (45 ml) melted coconut oil

2 tbsp (30 ml) pure maple syrup

1 tbsp (15 ml) fresh lemon juice

½ tsp pumpkin pie spice

Coconut Whipped Cream (page 100; optional), for topping

Line the bottom of an 8-inch (20-cm) round cake pan with parchment paper and grease the sides.

To make the crust, place the almonds and coconut in a food processor and pulse a few times, until the ingredients are crumbly. Add the dates, cinnamon, salt and milk and process until a sticky dough forms. Transfer the crust mixture to the prepared cake pan and press it down evenly.

To make the cream layer, combine the cashews, coconut cream, oil, maple syrup, pumpkin pie spice and lemon juice in a high-speed blender. Blend on high for 1 to 2 minutes, until the mixture is smooth. Pour this cream layer over the crust and make sure the layer is completely even. Freeze for 1 hour.

In the meantime, prepare the pumpkin layer. Combine the cashews, coconut cream, pumpkin puree, oil, maple syrup, lemon juice and pumpkin pie spice in the high-speed blender and blend on high until smooth. Then, once the cream layer has set in the freezer, pour the pumpkin layer on top and spread it out evenly. Return the cheesecake to the freezer for 2 to 3 hours, until it is completely firm. Slice the cheesecake and serve with a dollop of the Coconut Whipped Cream (if using).

SPICED PUMPKIN CREAM ROLL

This pumpkin-infused cream roll is the perfect cake for hosting fall gatherings.
Filled with warming spices, this fluffy cake roll will surely wow your friends.

YIELD: 10 servings

CAKE

1½ cups (173 g) spelt flour

¼ cup (48 g) coconut sugar

3 tbsp (24 g) cornstarch

½ tsp baking powder

½ tsp baking soda

½ tsp ground cinnamon

¼ tsp ground cloves

¼ tsp ground ginger

¼ tsp ground cardamom

¼ tsp ground nutmeg

Pinch of salt

1½ cups (338 g) pumpkin puree

2 tbsp (30 ml) pure maple syrup

3 tbsp (45 ml) melted coconut oil

½ tsp pure vanilla extract

Powdered sugar, as needed (optional)

CREAM FILLING

1 (14-oz [420-ml]) can full-fat
coconut cream, refrigerated
overnight

1 tbsp (15 ml) pure maple syrup

1 tsp pure vanilla extract

To make the cake, preheat the oven to 350°F (175°C) and line a 9½ x 12½–inch (24 x 32–cm) baking sheet with parchment paper, making sure the edges are completely covered. (Note that it's important to use a baking sheet that's close to these dimensions, or the cake will be too thick or thin to roll.)

In a large bowl, combine the flour, coconut sugar, cornstarch, baking powder, baking soda, cinnamon, cloves, ginger, cardamom, nutmeg and salt. In a medium bowl, combine the pumpkin puree, maple syrup, oil and vanilla. Pour the pumpkin mixture into the flour mixture and stir until just combined. The batter should be thick and pourable.

Transfer the batter to the prepared baking sheet and spread it into an even layer. It should be about ½ inch (13 mm) thick. Bake the cake for 10 to 12 minutes, or until a toothpick inserted into the center comes out clean. Let the cake cool for about 3 minutes. Then gently roll the cake from short end to short end, rolling up the parchment paper inside the cake and using it as a guide. Be very careful with this step so as not to break the cake, and try to handle it as little as possible. Let the cake cool to room temperature, about 30 minutes (otherwise the filling will melt).

While the cake is cooling, make the cream filling. Quickly rinse the medium bowl and scoop only the solid portion of the chilled coconut cream into the bowl. Add the maple syrup and vanilla. Whip the cream using a hand mixer until light and fluffy, 1 to 2 minutes, and transfer the bowl to the fridge.

Once the cake has cooled to room temperature, carefully unroll it and top it with all of the cream filling. Spread the cream filling evenly over the cake, leaving a ½-inch (13-mm) border along the edge. Begin rolling the cake back up the same way it was unrolled, from short end to short end, removing the parchment paper as you go. Continue rolling, using the parchment paper as a guide, until the cake is seam-side down. Wipe away any excess filling that may have spilled over.

Gently wrap the cake in parchment paper and carefully transfer it to a cutting board and refrigerate it until it is completely chilled and firm enough to handle easily, 1 to 2 hours. Leave the cake as is or dust it with the powdered sugar (if using).

PUMPKIN PIE WITH CRUNCHY PECAN STREUSEL

What would Thanksgiving be without pumpkin pie? Just give me a huge piece of this rich, warmly spiced pumpkin goodness with a dollop of whipped coconut cream and I'm a happy gal! This masterpiece comes with a delicious pecan streusel to add that extra sweet crunch.

YIELD: 8 servings

CRUST

2 cups (230 g) spelt flour

1 tbsp (12 g) coconut sugar

Pinch of salt

⅓ cup (75 g) vegan butter

¼ cup (60 ml) vegetable oil

5 to 6 tbsp (75 to 90 ml) cold water

FILLING

2 cups (450 g) pumpkin puree

¼ cup (60 ml) pure maple syrup

2 tbsp (22 g) almond butter

¾ cup (180 ml) full-fat coconut cream

3 tbsp (36 g) coconut sugar

1½ tsp (5 g) pumpkin pie spice

4 tbsp (32 g) cornstarch

½ cup (75 g) raw cashews

1 tsp pure vanilla extract

Pinch of salt

PECAN STREUSEL

1 cup (120 g) raw pecans, finely chopped

1 tbsp (15 ml) pure maple syrup

2 tbsp (24 g) coconut sugar

2 tbsp (30 ml) melted coconut oil

To make the crust, whisk together the flour, sugar and salt in a large bowl. Add the butter and vegetable oil and mix with an electric hand mixer fitted with kneading hooks until a crumbly dough forms, 2 to 3 minutes. Add the water little by little until the mixture starts to form a dough that holds together. Using your hands, knead the dough for 1 minute, until it forms a smooth ball. Wrap the dough in plastic wrap and chill it in the fridge for 30 minutes.

Preheat the oven to 350°F (175°C) and grease a deep 10½-inch (27-cm) pie dish.

While the oven preheats, make the filling. In a high-speed blender, combine the pumpkin puree, maple syrup, almond butter, cream, sugar, pumpkin pie spice, cornstarch, cashews, vanilla and salt and blend for 1 to 2 minutes on high, until the filling is completely smooth. Set the filling aside.

To make the pecan streusel, combine the pecans, maple syrup, sugar and oil in a food processor and pulse until the mixture is crumbly and moist.

(continued)

PUMPKIN PIE WITH CRUNCHY PECAN STREUSEL (CONTINUED)

TOPPING

Coconut whipped cream (see Quick Tip)

On a floured work surface, roll out the dough into a circle slightly larger than the prepared pie dish. Carefully roll the dough over the rolling pin and transfer it to the pie dish. Press the dough into the sides of the dish and trim the edges. Pour the filling into the dough and spread it out evenly with a spatula. Bake the pie for 20 minutes, then remove it and crumble the pecan streusel on top. Bake for another 30 minutes, until the pie is golden brown (cover it with foil if it starts to brown too quickly).

Let the pie cool completely and place it in the fridge to set for 1 hour before slicing. Serve with coconut whipped cream and reheat for 5 minutes if desired.

QUICK TIP: Coconut whipped cream is a great vegan alternative to the heavy, dairy-based whipped cream. Simply place a 14-ounce (420-ml) can of full-fat coconut cream in the fridge overnight so that the fat content firms up. Scoop the firm coconut cream into a medium bowl, add 1 teaspoon of pure vanilla extract and 1 tablespoon (15 ml) of pure maple syrup and whisk together with an electric hand mixer until it is light and fluffy, 1 to 2 minutes. Place the whipped cream in the fridge for 1 hour and serve. You can freeze the leftover coconut water from the can of coconut cream into ice cubes and use them for smoothies.

GLUTEN-FREE SUBSTITUTE: To make this recipe gluten free, follow the note in the recipe for Sweet Potato Gnocchi in Sage Butter (page 84).

CINNAMON APPLE PIE

Because I grew up in Germany, a good apple pie has always had a special place in my heart. This beautiful vegan version of the classic apple pie not only brings out a festive touch with wonderful spices, but its braided elements add a surprising twist to a family favorite. Get playful and go crazy with festive cookie cutters and braiding techniques for some extra fun!

YIELD: 8 servings

CRUST

3 cups (345 g) spelt flour

1 tbsp (12 g) coconut sugar

Pinch of salt

½ cup (113 g) vegan butter

⅓ cup (80 ml) vegetable oil

6 to 10 tbsp (90 to 150 ml) cold water

FILLING

6 medium apples (any variety), peeled, cored, halved and cut into thin slices

2 tbsp (30 ml) fresh lemon juice

1 tbsp (8 g) ground cinnamon

1 tsp ground ginger

2 tbsp (16 g) cornstarch

CARAMEL SAUCE

4 tbsp (56 g) vegan butter

½ cup (96 g) coconut sugar

4 tbsp (60 ml) full-fat coconut cream

1 tsp pure vanilla extract

To make the crust, whisk together the flour, sugar and salt in a large bowl. Add the butter and oil and mix with an electric hand mixer fitted with kneading hooks until you have a crumbly dough. Add the water little by little until a dough begins to form. Using your hands, knead the dough for 1 minute, until it forms a smooth ball. Wrap the dough in plastic wrap and chill it in the fridge for 30 minutes.

In the meantime, make the filling. Place the apple slices in a large bowl and toss them with the lemon juice to prevent them from browning. Add the cinnamon, ginger and cornstarch and toss until the apples are evenly coated. Transfer the apples to a large saucepan over medium heat and cook for 4 to 5 minutes, until they are slightly softened, then remove the saucepan from the heat.

Preheat the oven to 350°F (175°C) and grease a deep 10½-inch (27-cm) pie dish.

While the oven preheats, make the caramel sauce. Melt the butter in a small saucepan over medium heat and add the sugar, coconut cream and vanilla. Bring the mixture to a boil, reduce the heat to medium-low and simmer for 2 minutes, until it creates a creamy caramel. Pour half of the sauce over the apples, making sure they are evenly coated. Set the rest of the caramel sauce aside for serving.

On a floured work surface, roll half of the dough into a circle slightly larger than the prepared pie dish. Carefully roll the dough over the rolling pin and transfer it to the pie dish. Press the dough into the sides of the pie dish and trim the edges.

Fill the dough with the apple-caramel mixture and spread it out evenly.

(continued)

CINNAMON-SUGAR TOPPING

½ tsp coconut sugar

¼ tsp ground cinnamon

Roll out the other half of the dough so that it's the same size as the half holding the apple filling. Cut it into 1-inch (2.5-cm)-thick strips. Lay the strips on top of the pie in a lattice design: Lay out 8 parallel strips of the pie dough on top of the filling, with about ½ inch (13 mm) of space between them. Fold back every other strip. Place one long strip of dough perpendicular to the parallel strips. Unfold the folded strips over the perpendicular strip. Now take the parallel strips that are running underneath the perpendicular strip and fold them back over the perpendicular strip. Lay down a second perpendicular strip of dough next to the first strip. Unfold the folded parallel strips over the second strip. Continue this process until the weave is complete over the top of the pie.

Trim the edges of the strips. Trim the sides of the dough and use any leftovers to make decorations with cookie cutters, placing the shapes on top of the lattice crust.

To make the cinnamon-sugar topping, combine the sugar and cinnamon in a small bowl.

Brush the pie with a bit of the caramel sauce and sprinkle the crust with the cinnamon-sugar topping. Bake the pie for 40 to 45 minutes, covering the pie with foil if it starts to brown too much. Serve the pie with the remaining caramel sauce while it's still warm.

POACHED PEAR CHAI BREAD

This elegant version of a sunken pear cake is true to its flavors and hides the perfect surprise on the inside, making it incredibly moist and fluffy. This bread gets a powerful infusion of fresh ginger, maple syrup and white wine to make it even more festive.

YIELD: 8 servings

POACHED PEARS

2 medium pears (any variety)

2½ cups (600 ml) water

1 tsp pure maple syrup

1 tsp grated fresh ginger

½ cup (120 ml) dry white wine

CAKE

1 tbsp (7 g) ground flaxseed

3 tbsp (45 ml) water

1 cup (240 ml) almond or soy milk

1 tbsp (15 ml) apple cider vinegar

⅓ cup (80 ml) melted coconut oil

¼ cup (60 ml) date syrup

½ cup (113 g) pumpkin puree

2 cups (230 g) spelt flour

1 tbsp (11 g) baking powder

½ cup (96 g) coconut sugar

1 tsp ground cinnamon

1 tsp ground ginger

½ tsp ground nutmeg

½ tsp ground cloves

¼ tsp ground cardamom

Pinch of salt

ORANGE GLAZE

Juice of 1 orange, or as needed

½ cup (65 g) powdered sugar

To make the poached pears, slice the bottoms off the pears and peel them, leaving the stems attached. In a medium pot over high heat, bring the water, maple syrup, ginger and wine (if using) to a boil Place the pears in the pot so that they stand upright and reduce the heat to medium-low. Simmer for 6 to 7 minutes, until the pears are just tender, then carefully remove them from the pot and set aside.

Preheat the oven to 350°F (175°C) and line a 9 x 5–inch (23 x 13–cm) loaf pan with parchment paper.

To make the cake, make a flax egg by combining the flaxseed with the water in a small bowl. Set the mixture aside and let it thicken.

In a large bowl, combine the milk with the vinegar and let the milk curdle for 5 minutes to create vegan buttermilk. Add the oil, date syrup, pumpkin puree and flax egg and combine.

In another large bowl, whisk together the flour, baking powder, coconut sugar, cinnamon, ginger, nutmeg, cloves, cardamom and salt. Pour the buttermilk mixture into the flour mixture and beat with an electric mixer on low speed until just combined (don't overmix). Pour the batter into the prepared loaf pan and gently place the pears inside so that they are standing upright, surrounded by the batter. Bake, covered, for 35 minutes. Uncover the loaf pan and bake for another 10 minutes. Let the bread cool slightly before transferring it to a wire rack to finish cooling.

To make the orange glaze, combine the orange juice and powdered sugar in a small bowl and mix until smooth and pourable. (Add more or less orange juice depending on the desired consistency.) Drizzle the glaze on top of the bread and serve while it's still warm.

NUTTY FUDGE BROWNIES

These might just be the fudgiest brownies I've created so far! Apart from being incredibly rich, they are filled with crunchy walnut pieces and boast a fruity and creamy layer on top. This recipe is a beloved family favorite that is nutritious, naturally sweetened and absolutely delicious! • **GLUTEN FREE** •

YIELD: 12 to 14 servings

BERRY-CHIA JAM

1 cup (155 g) frozen blueberries or raspberries

½ tsp fresh lemon juice

2 tbsp (30 ml) pure maple syrup

½ tsp pure vanilla extract

4 tbsp (40 g) chia seeds

BROWNIES

20 Medjool dates, pitted

1 medium ripe avocado

½ cup (120 ml) almond or soy milk

2 tbsp (30 ml) melted coconut oil

1 tsp pure vanilla extract

Pinch of salt

½ cup (56 g) cacao powder

¾ cup (72 g) almond flour

½ cup (60 g) raw walnuts, roughly chopped

1 tsp baking powder

⅓ cup (60 g) 70% cacao vegan dark chocolate chips

NUTTY SWIRL

2 tbsp (22 g) nut butter of choice

2 tbsp (30 ml) pure maple syrup

To make the berry-chia jam, heat a medium saucepan over medium heat and add the blueberries. Add the lemon juice and cook until the blueberries are soft, 4 to 5 minutes. Transfer them to a medium bowl and mash them with a potato masher if you like a chunky texture or blend them in a blender for a few seconds if you prefer a smooth texture. Add the maple syrup, vanilla and chia seeds and stir until well combined. Let the jam cool, then transfer it to a jar and store it in the fridge.

Preheat the oven to 350°F (175°C). Line an 8 x 8–inch (20 x 20–cm) baking pan with parchment paper.

To make the brownies, combine the dates, avocado, milk, oil, vanilla and salt to a food processor or high-speed blender and process until a smooth paste forms. Transfer the paste to a large bowl and add the cacao powder, flour, walnuts, baking powder and chocolate chips. Use a spatula to mix everything together into a smooth, sticky batter.

Scoop the batter into the prepared baking pan and spread it out evenly with a wet spoon.

To make the nutty swirl, combine the nut butter and maple syrup in a small bowl. Place the nutty swirl, as well as the berry-chia jam, on top of the batter. Use a toothpick to draw swirls in the batter.

Bake the brownies for 20 to 25 minutes, until they are golden brown on top. Let the brownies cool completely, then place them in the fridge for a minimum of 2 hours (overnight is best). Cut the brownies into squares and serve.

CHOCOLATE MOUSSE PIE

This super easy chocolate mousse pie has got to be one of my absolute favorite desserts ever! It's rich, chocolaty and silky smooth—three things I adore in desserts. The filling is undetectably dairy free and has been raved about by my nonvegan friends. The pie can be served fully chilled or frozen, but personally I prefer the smooth touch of a slightly chilled piece of this gorgeous pie. • GLUTEN FREE •

YIELD: 8 servings

CRUST

1½ cups (180 g) raw walnuts

1½ cups (225 g) dried figs, roughly chopped

FILLING

12 oz (336 g) silken tofu, drained

½ cup (113 g) solid chilled full-fat coconut cream

5 oz (140 g) 70% cacao dark vegan chocolate, melted

3 tbsp (45 ml) pure maple syrup

3 tbsp (21 g) cacao powder

2 tbsp (22 g) almond butter

½ tsp pure vanilla extract

COCONUT WHIPPED CREAM

1 (14-oz [420-ml]) can full-fat coconut cream, refrigerated overnight

1 tbsp (15 ml) pure maple syrup

1 tsp pure vanilla extract

Grease a 9-inch (23-cm) tart pan with a removable bottom.

To make the crust, place the walnuts in a food processor and pulse a few times, until they are crumbly. Add the figs and blend until the mixture is moist and chunky.

Transfer the crust mixture to the prepared tart pan. Use your fingers to spread it evenly across the bottom and sides of the pan.

To make the filling, combine the tofu, coconut cream, chocolate, maple syrup, cacao powder, almond butter and vanilla in a high-speed blender and blend for 1 to 2 minutes, until the filling is completely smooth. Pour the filling into the tart pan and even out the top. Place the tart pan in the freezer for 1 to 2 hours, until the filling is set. After the filling has set, chill the pie overnight in the fridge for a silky smooth consistency or keep it in the freezer for a firmer texture.

To make the coconut whipped cream, scoop only the solid portion of the chilled coconut cream into a small bowl. Add the maple syrup and vanilla and whip with an electric hand mixer until it is light and fluffy, 1 to 2 minutes. Serve the pie with a dollop of the coconut whipped cream on top.

QUICK TIP: Tofu, despite its bad reputation, can be extremely healthy for you and has many benefits. It's high in protein, low in fat and has the perfect texture to achieve silky, creamy results in many plant-based desserts!

Colorful
EASTER TABLE

Spring is in the air and the flowers are blooming!

For me, Easter is all about hours-long brunches with the entire family. Turns out, we vegans don't have to give up all the things we love about eggy Easter foods after all, thanks to kala namak (aka Himalayan black salt), which has a distinctive eggy flavor.

In the following pages, you'll find anything from freshly baked Cinnamon Hot Cross Buns (page 129) to Vegan Egg Salad (page 117) to Sweet Onion and Asparagus Quiche (page 118) to hearty Dijon Scalloped Potatoes (page 114), as well as the impressive Carrot Cake with Vanilla Cream Frosting (page 133) and Almond-Mocha Torte (page 127).

The Marzipan Challah (page 56) and Balsamic-Roasted Beetroot Salad with Almond Feta (page 69) from the previous chapters will also fit in perfectly on your Easter table, so make sure to revisit them. Now off to the kitchen!

CHICKPEA-LEEK FRITTATA

As far as Easter traditions go, waking up to the smell of a freshly baked breakfast frittata has to be on the top of the list! This Chickpea-Leek Frittata is not only crustless but also egg free. It's filling, moist on the inside, loaded with veggies and super delicious and has quickly become one of our family favorites because it's nutritious and easy to make. • GLUTEN FREE •

YIELD: 8 servings

1 cup (90 g) chickpea flour

2 tbsp (10 g) nutritional yeast

1 cup (240 ml) vegetable broth

¾ cup (180 ml) water

¼ cup (60 ml) cashew cream or cashew milk

½ tsp ground turmeric

½ tsp kala namak (Himalayan black salt) (see Quick Tip)

2 tbsp (30 ml) olive oil

1 medium red onion, thinly sliced

1½ cups (135 g) thinly sliced leeks

2 cloves garlic, minced

1 cup (30 g) fresh spinach, roughly chopped

Spring onions, chopped, for serving

Preheat the oven to 350°F (175°C) and grease a 9-inch (23-cm) tart pan with a removable bottom.

In a high-speed blender, combine the flour, nutritional yeast, broth, water, cashew cream, turmeric and kala namak and blend for 1 minute, until the mixture is smooth.

Heat the oil in a medium saucepan over medium heat. Add the onion and leeks and sauté until they are translucent, 4 to 5 minutes. Add the garlic and spinach and cook for 2 minutes. Transfer half of the vegetables to the prepared tart pan and spread them out evenly. Pour the flour mixture on top and spread it out evenly. Spread out the remaining vegetables evenly on top and bake for 45 to 50 minutes.

Let the frittata cool for 10 minutes before slicing. Serve with spring onions and your favorite vegan dip on top.

QUICK TIP: Kala namak, also known as Himalayan black salt, is a rock salt used in South Asian cuisine. It has a sulfurous, eggy smell and is widely used in the plant-based kitchen to imitate the flavor of eggs.

DIJON SCALLOPED POTATOES

Scalloped potatoes are the perfect creamy side (or main) dish for a special occasion, but they truly shine for Easter. This recipe is incredibly easy to make and yields a wonderfully cheesy dish of hearty potato goodness. I assure you that you'll fall in love with this after eating it the first time, and it'll become a staple in your household—as it has in mine! • GLUTEN FREE •

YIELD: 6 servings

CREAMY SAUCE

1 cup (150 g) raw cashews, soaked 6 to 8 hours (or overnight) and drained

1 cup (240 ml) vegetable broth

1½ cups (360 ml) almond milk

1 tbsp (16 g) Dijon mustard

½ cup (40 g) nutritional yeast

½ tsp salt

¼ tsp black pepper

⅛ tsp ground nutmeg

POTATOES

2 tbsp (30 ml) olive oil

1 large white onion, thickly sliced

3 cloves garlic, minced

4 medium Yukon gold potatoes, peeled and thinly sliced

TOPPING

Vegan Parmesan (page 76), as needed

Fresh chives, finely chopped

Preheat the oven to 350°F (175°C) and grease a 7 x 10–inch (18 x 25–cm) baking dish.

To make the creamy sauce, combine the cashews, broth, milk, mustard, nutritional yeast, salt, black pepper and nutmeg in a high-speed blender. Blend for 1 to 2 minutes, until the mixture is smooth.

To make the potatoes, heat the olive oil in a medium skillet over medium heat. Add the onion and sauté until it is translucent, 3 to 4 minutes. Add the garlic and cook for 1 minute.

Pour a thin layer of the creamy sauce into the prepared baking dish and spread it out evenly. Place a layer of the potatoes on the sauce, then top the potatoes with a layer of the onion-garlic mixture and add more creamy sauce until they are just covered. Repeat these steps until all the ingredients are gone, finishing with an even layer of the sauce.

Cover the baking dish with aluminum foil and bake for 1 hour. Let the potatoes cool for 10 minutes, top them with the Vegan Parmesan and chives and serve.

VEGAN EGG SALAD

During Easter, most brunch tables are filled with rich egg salads that use leftover eggs. Because we don't want to miss out on all the fun, having a super easy vegan egg salad recipe is crucial. This dish is not only much healthier than the original but it's also full of plant-based protein and makes a great breakfast or lunch recipe. • **GLUTEN FREE** •

YIELD: 4 servings

MAYONNAISE

⅓ cup (80 ml) sunflower oil

3 tbsp (45 ml) soy milk

¼ tsp ground turmeric

1 tsp Dijon mustard

1 tsp kala namak (Himalayan black salt)

EGG SALAD

7 oz (196 g) medium-firm tofu, drained and pressed 5 to 10 minutes

½ medium red onion, diced

2 tbsp (6 g) finely chopped green onions

1 tbsp (3 g) finely chopped fresh dill (optional)

1 tbsp (3 g) finely chopped fresh chives

1 tsp white wine vinegar

¼ cup (25 g) finely chopped celery

Black pepper, to taste

Kala namak (Himalayan black salt), to taste

To make the mayonnaise, combine the oil, milk, turmeric, mustard and kala namak in a narrow glass jar. Use an immersion blender to blend the ingredients for 30 to 60 seconds, until they are creamy. Add more milk to make it smoother or more oil to make it firmer.

Roughly chop the tofu into chunks, then transfer them to a medium bowl. Add the mayonnaise, onion, green onions, dill (if using), chives, vinegar, celery and black pepper and stir gently until the ingredients are well incorporated. Add additional black pepper and the kala namak. Serve as desired.

SWEET ONION AND ASPARAGUS QUICHE

A beautiful veggie quiche should be part of any great Easter brunch. As asparagus is just in season, this quiche combines a delicious, cheesy filling with tons of balsamic-maple roasted vegetables for that extra zing.

YIELD: 8 servings

ONION AND ASPARAGUS

1 tbsp (15 ml) olive oil

1 large red onion, thinly sliced

2 cloves garlic

7 oz (196 g) green asparagus, trimmed and roughly chopped

1 tbsp (15 ml) pure maple syrup

1 tsp balsamic vinegar

1 sheet vegan puff pastry, thawed

FILLING

7 oz (196 g) silken tofu, drained

3 tbsp (15 g) nutritional yeast

5 to 6 sun-dried tomatoes (see Quick Tip)

2 tbsp (16 g) cornstarch

¼ cup (60 ml) soy milk

¼ tsp salt

¼ tsp black pepper

Preheat the oven to 350°F (175°C) and grease a 9-inch (23-cm) tart pan with a removable bottom.

To make the onion and asparagus, heat the oil in a medium saucepan over medium heat. Add the onion and sauté until it is translucent, 3 to 4 minutes. Add the garlic, asparagus, maple syrup and vinegar and cook for 2 to 3 minutes.

Place the sheet of puff pastry in the prepared tart pan and press down on the bottom and sides. Trim the remaining pastry from the sides of the pan.

To make the filling, combine the tofu, nutritional yeast, tomatoes, cornstarch, milk, salt and black pepper in a high-speed blender. Blend for 1 minute, until the mixture is smooth. Pour the filling into the tart pan and spread it out evenly. Distribute the onion-asparagus mixture on top. Bake for 25 to 30 minutes, until the pastry is golden brown. Let the quiche cool for 10 minutes, then place it in the fridge to set for 1 hour before serving.

QUICK TIP: You can use either jarred sun-dried tomatoes packaged in oil or dehydrated ones that come in a bag. If you choose the dehydrated variety, soak them in 1 cup (240 ml) of hot water for 5 minutes before using.

SPINACH AND MUSHROOM ALFREDO LASAGNA

Forget the time-consuming task of presoaking lasagna noodles and the hours of preparation.
A quick whiz in the blender, a few minutes to sauté veggies and just moments to prepare the sauce
and you're ready to go.

YIELD: 6 to 8 servings

CASHEW BÉCHAMEL SAUCE

1½ cups (225 g) raw cashews, soaked 6 to 8 hours (or overnight) and drained

⅓ cup (27 g) nutritional yeast

2 tsp (10 ml) fresh lemon juice

1 tsp garlic powder

1 tsp onion powder

⅓ cup (80 ml) water, plus more as needed

Dash of salt

Dash of black pepper

LASAGNA

3 tbsp (45 ml) olive oil

1 medium white onion, diced

3 cups (225 g) thinly sliced cremini or white button mushrooms

3 cups (90 g) fresh spinach

4 cloves garlic, minced

½ tsp salt

½ tsp black pepper

12 oven-ready lasagna noodles

Vegan Parmesan (page 76), as needed

Preheat the oven to 350°F (175°C) and grease a 7 x 10–inch (18 x 25–cm) baking dish.

To make the cashew béchamel sauce, combine the cashews, nutritional yeast, lemon juice, garlic powder, onion powder, water, salt and black pepper in a high-speed blender. Blend for 1 to 2 minutes, until the mixture is smooth. Set aside.

To make the lasagna, heat the oil in a large saucepan over medium heat. Add the onion and sauté until it is translucent, 3 to 4 minutes. Add the mushrooms and cook for 2 minutes, until they are soft. Add the spinach, garlic, salt and black pepper and cook for 2 minutes, until the spinach is soft. Take the saucepan off the heat and set aside.

(continued)

ALFREDO SAUCE

3 tbsp (42 g) vegan butter

4 tbsp (32 g) all-purpose flour

3 to 4 cups (720 to 960 ml) almond or soy milk

3 tbsp (15 g) nutritional yeast

1 tsp garlic powder

1 tsp salt

½ tsp black pepper

⅛ tsp ground nutmeg

To make the alfredo sauce, melt the butter in a medium saucepan over medium heat. Whisk in the flour until a paste forms. Slowly add the milk, about ½ cup (120 ml) at a time, whisking until there are no lumps. Add the nutritional yeast, garlic powder, salt, black pepper and nutmeg and bring the sauce to a simmer. Whisk constantly for about 3 minutes, until the sauce thickens, then take it off the heat.

Start layering the lasagna. Add a thin layer of the cashew béchamel sauce on the bottom of the prepared baking dish and spread it out evenly. Add a layer of the lasagna noodles, a layer of the béchamel sauce, a layer of the spinach-mushroom mixture and a layer of the alfredo sauce. Repeat this process until you run out of ingredients, topping the last layer of the lasagna with lasagna noodles and alfredo sauce. Sprinkle the lasagna with the Vegan Parmesan and bake for 25 to 30 minutes. Let the lasagna cool for 10 minutes before serving.

SPLIT PEA SOUP WITH TEMPEH BACON

This vegan split pea soup is the perfect warming meal on a chilly day, as well as the ideal addition to your Easter brunch—it's healthy, hearty and absolutely delicious! The addition of tempeh bacon adds a smoky flavor and switches up the textures. This soup is also inexpensive to make, and you can often feed the entire party for less than 10 bucks! • GLUTEN FREE •

YIELD: 6 servings

SOUP

1 tbsp (15 ml) olive oil

1 large white onion, diced

1 medium carrot, peeled and diced

4 cloves garlic, minced

5 cups (1.2 L) vegetable broth

2 cups (400 g) dried split peas, rinsed and soaked overnight

1 cup (240 ml) canned coconut milk

1 tbsp (15 ml) fresh lemon juice

Zest of ½ to 1 lemon

2 tbsp (10 g) nutritional yeast

1 tsp salt

1 tsp black pepper

TEMPEH BACON

8 oz (224 g) tempeh (see Quick Tip on page 124)

1½ tbsp (23 ml) soy sauce

1 tbsp (15 ml) sesame oil

3 tbsp (45 ml) water

1 tbsp (15 ml) pure maple syrup

½ tsp paprika

½ tsp liquid smoke or ½ tsp smoked paprika

Pinch of black pepper

1 tsp olive oil

To make the soup, heat the olive oil in a large pot over medium heat. Add the onion and sauté until it is translucent, 3 to 4 minutes. Add the carrot and garlic and cook for 5 minutes, until the garlic is very fragrant. Add the broth and bring the mixture to a boil. Add the split peas and reduce the heat to medium-low. Simmer for 1½ to 2 hours, until the split peas are cooked through.

While the soup is cooking, prepare the tempeh bacon. Slice the tempeh into thin slices. In a small bowl, mix together the soy sauce, sesame oil, water, maple syrup, paprika, liquid smoke and black pepper. Soak the tempeh slices in the marinade for 2 minutes. Heat the olive oil in a medium skillet over high heat and add the tempeh slices. Cook for 1 minute on each side, until both sides are crisp. Remove the tempeh bacon from the heat and slice it into smaller pieces.

Once the soup is done cooking, add the coconut milk, lemon juice, lemon zest, nutritional yeast, salt and black pepper and combine. Use an immersion blender to blend the soup to the desired consistency. If you prefer a chunkier soup, reserve one-third of the soup and return it to the pot after blending the other two-thirds.

(continued)

TOPPING

Olive oil, as needed

½ cup (8 g) roughly chopped fresh cilantro

2 tbsp (12 g) toasted slivered almonds

Dash of paprika

Dash of red pepper flakes

½ tsp lemon zest

Top the soup with a drizzle of olive oil, the cilantro, almonds, paprika, red pepper flakes, lemon zest and tempeh bacon and serve.

QUICK TIP: Tempeh is a traditional soy product that originated in Indonesia. It is made by culturing and fermenting soybeans into a cake form. You'll find tempeh in most Asian supermarkets in the frozen section.

GLUTEN-FREE SUBSTITUTION: To make this recipe gluten free, follow the note in the recipe for Hearty Shepherd's Pie (page 20).

ALMOND-MOCHA TORTE

Nothing reminds me more of Easter brunch than a decadent mocha torte. This scrumptious almond-mocha torte is the perfect luscious cake for special occasions and will surely leave your guests with tasty memories! The cake layers are light and airy thanks to the use of aquafaba, and they're smothered in layers of creamy mocha frosting. Are you drooling yet?

YIELD: 10 servings

ALMOND SPONGE CAKE

1 cup (240 ml) aquafaba (see Quick Tip on page 61)

2 tsp (10 ml) almond extract

4 tbsp (60 ml) melted coconut oil

Vegan butter, as needed

2 cups (192 g) almond flour

1½ cups (180 g) all-purpose flour

1 cup (192 g) coconut sugar

2 tsp (8 g) baking powder

½ tsp baking soda

½ cup (120 ml) almond milk

2 tsp (10 ml) apple cider vinegar

Chocolate shavings, as needed

Slivered almonds, as needed

MOCHA BUTTERCREAM FILLING

4 tbsp (56 g) vegan butter

1 cup (130 g) powdered sugar

2 tbsp (14 g) cacao powder

2 tbsp (30 ml) espresso or black coffee

To make the almond sponge cake, place the aquafaba in a medium glass bowl and put the bowl in the fridge to chill for 15 minutes. Once the aquafaba is chilled, use a stand or electric hand mixer to beat the aquafaba on high until stiff peaks form, 5 to 10 minutes. (Note that aquafaba can't be overbeaten, so it's fine to beat it a bit longer if needed.)

Add the almond extract and oil and beat for 1 to 2 minutes. The aquafaba will get thicker and shiny and quadruple in volume. It's done when you can turn the bowl upside down and the aquafaba stays in place.

Preheat the oven to 350°F (175°C). Line 3 (8-inch [20-cm]) round cake pans with parchment paper and grease them with butter.

In a large bowl, whisk together the almond flour, all-purpose flour, coconut sugar, baking powder and baking soda. Gently fold the aquafaba meringue into the flour mixture and add the milk and vinegar. Stir until just combined (do not overmix). Divide the batter between the 3 prepared cake pans and spread it out evenly. Shake each pan and tap it gently on the counter to ensure the batter is very even.

Bake the cakes for 20 to 25 minutes, or until a toothpick inserted into the centers comes out clean. Remove the cakes from the pans and let them cool on a wire rack.

To make the mocha buttercream filling, place the butter in a medium bowl. Beat the butter with an electric hand mixer until it is smooth. Add the powdered sugar and cacao powder and continue beating. While beating the butter mixture, add 1 tablespoon (15 ml) of the espresso. Continue beating and add the remaining 1 tablespoon (15 ml) of espresso while beating the mixture until it's smooth.

(continued)

GANACHE

2 cups (450 g) solid chilled coconut cream

2 tbsp (14 g) cacao powder

1 tsp almond or pure vanilla extract

2 tbsp (30 ml) pure maple syrup

To make the ganache, place the coconut cream, cacao powder, almond extract and maple syrup in a medium bowl and beat with an electric hand mixer until the mixture is smooth. Place the ganache in the fridge for 30 minutes to firm up.

Place the first cake layer on a serving platter. Add a layer of the mocha buttercream filling on top and spread it out evenly. Add the second cake layer, another mocha buttercream layer and add the third cake layer. Apply the ganache and use a frosting knife to form a thick layer all around the cake. Decorate the cake with the chocolate shavings and slivered almonds on top. Refrigerate the cake until ready to serve.

CINNAMON HOT CROSS BUNS

Bake up a batch of these fluffy, perfectly spiced cinnamon hot cross buns to make your Easter celebration complete. These gorgeous buns will make your entire house smell heavenly and are so good that you'll want to make them all year-round!

YIELD: 12 servings

DOUGH

1 (¼-oz [7-g]) packet instant yeast

½ cup (120 ml) warm water

1 tsp granulated sugar

2 tbsp (30 ml) vegetable oil

2 tbsp (30 g) unsweetened applesauce

½ cup (120 ml) almond milk

2 cups (230 g) spelt flour

2 cups (240 g) all-purpose flour, divided

4 tbsp (48 g) coconut sugar

1 tbsp (8 g) ground cinnamon

½ tsp ground nutmeg

1 tbsp (6 g) lemon zest

1 tbsp (6 g) orange zest

1 tsp salt

¾ cup (113 g) raisins

To make the dough, combine the yeast, water and granulated sugar in a small bowl and let the mixture rest for 3 minutes. Add the oil, applesauce and milk and mix slightly.

In the bowl of a stand mixer fitted with dough hooks, combine the spelt flour, 1½ cups (180 g) of the all-purpose flour, coconut sugar, cinnamon, nutmeg, lemon zest, orange zest and salt. Add the liquid yeast mixture and set the mixer to knead. Let the mixer knead for 4 minutes, until the dough is no longer sticky (if you don't have a stand mixer, simply knead the dough by hand). If the dough is still sticky, add the remaining ½ cup (60 g) of all-purpose flour a little bit at a time until the dough is no longer sticky. During the last minute of kneading, add the raisins.

Lightly grease a large bowl and transfer the dough to the bowl. Cover the bowl with a towel and let the dough rise for 1 to 2 hours, until it has doubled in size.

Line a medium baking sheet with parchment paper. Punch the dough down and knead for 10 seconds to get rid of any air pockets. Divide the dough into 12 equal pieces and roll each piece into a ball.

Preheat the oven to 400°F (200°C) and lay the dough balls on the baking sheet in a 3 x 4 grid, so that they just touch one another (they will merge as they expand). Cover the dough balls with a towel and let them rise for another 30 minutes, until they have doubled in size.

(continued)

VEGAN EGG WASH

1 tbsp (20 g) apricot jam

2 tbsp (30 ml) almond milk

1 tsp pure maple syrup

ICING

⅓ cup (43 g) powdered sugar

½ tsp pure vanilla extract

1 tsp almond milk

In the meantime, make the vegan egg wash by combining the jam, milk and maple syrup in a small bowl. Gently brush the top of each dough ball with the egg wash, then bake the buns for 15 to 20 minutes, until they are golden brown.

As soon as the buns are out of the oven, brush them with the remaining egg wash until they are shiny, then place them on a cooling rack.

To make the icing, combine the powdered sugar, vanilla and milk in a small bowl and whisk together. Transfer the icing to a piping bag, paint a cross on top of each bun and serve.

CARROT CAKE WITH VANILLA CREAM FROSTING

This vegan version of the Easter classic is the perfect dessert for springtime celebrations! It's packed with warm spices, incredibly moist and slathered in creamy vegan frosting—yum!

YIELD: 10 servings

CARROT CAKE

2 tbsp (14 g) ground flaxseed

6 tbsp (90 ml) water

¾ cup (180 ml) almond milk

1 tsp pure vanilla extract

¼ cup (60 ml) pure maple syrup

¼ cup (60 ml) vegetable oil

½ cup (113 g) canned crushed pineapple, drained

2 cups (240 g) all-purpose flour

1½ tsp (6 g) baking powder

1½ tsp (6 g) baking soda

1 tsp ground cinnamon

1 tsp ground ginger

½ tsp ground nutmeg

½ cup (96 g) coconut sugar

2 cups (220 g) peeled and grated carrots

½ cup (60 g) raw walnuts, roughly chopped

VANILLA CREAM FROSTING

2 (14-oz [420-ml]) cans full-fat coconut cream, refrigerated overnight

2 tbsp (30 ml) pure maple syrup

1 tsp pure vanilla extract

½ cup (60 g) raw walnuts, roughly chopped, for topping

Preheat the oven to 350°F (175°C) and line 2 (8-inch [20-cm]) round cake pans with parchment paper.

To make the carrot cake, make flax eggs by combining the flaxseed with the water in a small bowl. Set aside and let the mixture thicken.

In a large bowl, combine the milk, vanilla, maple syrup, oil and pineapple. In another large bowl, whisk together the flour, baking powder, baking soda, cinnamon, ginger, nutmeg, sugar, carrots and walnuts and whisk together. Add the flax eggs to the milk mixture, then pour the milk mixture into the flour mixture and use a spatula to carefully combine (do not overmix). Divide the batter between the 2 prepared cake pans and spread it out evenly. Bake the cakes for 35 to 40 minutes, until a toothpick inserted into the centers comes out clean. Remove the cakes from the oven and let them cool for 5 minutes. Remove the cakes from their pans and carefully transfer them to a wire rack to cool completely.

While the cakes are cooling, make the vanilla cream frosting. Scoop only the solid portion of the chilled coconut cream into a medium bowl. Add the syrup and vanilla and beat with an electric hand mixer until the frosting is smooth and creamy. Place the frosting in the fridge for 30 minutes to firm up.

Once the cakes have cooled completely, place one cake layer on a serving platter. Add a layer of frosting on top and spread it out evenly. Add the other cake layer and apply the rest of the frosting. Use a frosting knife to form a thick layer all around the cake. Decorate the top of the cake with the roughly chopped walnuts and refrigerate until ready to serve.

STRAWBERRY CUSTARD TART

For me, Easter is all about those luscious pastries filled with thick layers of custard and my favorite seasonal fruits. Personally, I don't think there is any better flavor combination than vanilla custard and strawberries. This tart is perfect for any occasion and specifically for your Easter table.

YIELD: 8 servings

CRUST

1 cup (120 g) all-purpose flour

Pinch of salt

⅓ cup (75 g) vegan butter

1 tbsp (15 ml) cold water

CUSTARD FILLING

½ cup (64 g) cornstarch

⅛ tsp ground turmeric

½ cup (120 ml) almond milk, divided

1 (14-oz [420-ml]) can full-fat coconut cream

⅓ cup (80 ml) pure maple syrup

1 tsp pure vanilla extract

TOPPING

5 to 6 strawberries, finely chopped

1 tbsp (12 g) granulated sugar

To make the crust, whisk together the flour and salt in a large bowl. Add the butter and mix with an electric hand mixer fitted with kneading hooks for 3 minutes, until a crumbly dough forms. Add the water and knead with the hand mixer until the dough comes together, about 2 minutes. Using your hands, knead the dough for 30 seconds until a smooth ball forms. Wrap the dough in plastic wrap and place it in the fridge for 30 minutes.

While the dough chills, preheat the oven to 350°F (175°C). Grease a 9-inch (23-cm) tart pan with a removable bottom.

On a floured work surface, roll out the dough into a circle slightly larger than the tart pan. Carefully roll the pastry over the rolling pin and transfer it to the prepared tart pan. Press the pastry into the sides of the pan and trim the edges. Line the top of the pastry with parchment paper, fill the crust completely with dried beans (ensuring that they are pressing on the sides as well as the bottom) and bake for 10 minutes. Remove the beans and parchment paper and bake for another 5 minutes. Set the crust aside to cool.

To make the custard filling, combine the cornstarch, turmeric and a splash of the milk in a small bowl and whisk until the mixture is smooth. Place the coconut cream, the remaining milk and the maple syrup in a medium saucepan over medium heat. Bring the milk mixture to a boil and slowly add the cornstarch mixture. Reduce the heat to low and whisk continuously to avoid burning or lumps. Add the vanilla and continue whisking for 3 to 4 minutes. When the mixture has thickened to a custard-like consistency, take it off the heat and pour it into the tart crust. Spread the custard out evenly and place the tart into the fridge to set for 1 hour.

To make the topping, combine the strawberries and sugar in a small saucepan over medium-high heat. Cook for 3 to 4 minutes, until the strawberries are soft and sticky. Spoon the topping on top of the custard layer and place the tart back in the fridge for at least 1 hour.

GLUTEN-FREE SUBSTITUTION: To make this recipe gluten free, follow the note for Fluffy Cornbread (page 92).

Festive
APPETIZERS & DRINKS

Whether you're looking for holiday hors d'oeuvres, festive finger foods or vegan versions of your favorite holiday drinks, you've come to the right place! From creamy vegan cheeses to dip platters to hearty soups and shareable bites, these appetizers are the perfect start to any holiday feast!

In addition to that, I chose to focus on my two favorite (and essential) holiday drinks. These celebratory beverages are loaded with flavors and a treat in and of themselves. They're great to pair with afternoon tea or some cookies or chocolate truffles. Or sip them along with your main course or the first thing in the morning. Both drinks are ridiculously easy to prepare and take only 10 to 15 minutes until they're ready to serve, so what are you waiting for?

NUTTY VEGAN CHEESEBALL

This beautiful vegan cheeseball is the ultimate festive appetizer. It is creamy, flavorful and perfect for any dairy-sensitive guests. You can easily make it a few days ahead of time and serve it with crackers or fresh vegetables just as your guests arrive. • **GLUTEN FREE** •

YIELD: 10 servings

CHEESEBALL

1 cup (134 g) raw macadamia nuts, soaked for 6 hours (or overnight) and drained

½ cup (75 g) raw cashews, soaked for 6 hours (or overnight) and drained

½ cup (120 ml) water

1½ tbsp (23 ml) fresh lemon juice

2 cloves garlic

1 tbsp (5 g) nutritional yeast

1 tbsp (15 ml) melted coconut oil

1 tsp Dijon mustard

½ tsp pure maple syrup

1 tsp dried thyme or rosemary

½ tsp salt

¼ tsp black pepper

COATING

¼ cup (30 g) raw pecans, finely chopped

1 tsp finely chopped fresh thyme

To make the cheeseball, place the macadamia nuts and cashews in a food processor or high-speed blender. Add the water, lemon juice, garlic, nutritional yeast, oil, mustard, maple syrup, thyme, salt and black pepper. Process until the mixture is very creamy and smooth, scraping down the sides and using the tamper tool as needed if using a blender. Taste and adjust the seasonings as needed.

Place a fine-mesh strainer over a medium bowl, and line the strainer with 2 layers of cheesecloth or a clean, fine-textured, absorbent towel. Transfer the cheeseball mixture to the cheesecloth. Gather the corners of the cheesecloth and twist the top gently to form the cheese into a ball. Secure the cheesecloth with an elastic band. Use your hands to squeeze out any extra liquid. Place the cheeseball in the fridge for 12 hours.

To make the coating, combine the pecans and thyme on a plate. Unwrap the cheeseball from the cheesecloth and place it on the plate. Use your hands to gently roll the ball around until it is coated on all sides. Once the cheeseball is fully coated, transfer it to a serving platter. Shape it with your hands as needed and arrange fresh vegetables and crackers around it. Store the cheeseball, covered, in the refrigerator for up to 4 days.

ROASTED PESTO MUSHROOMS

These flavorful mushrooms are a great appetizer or side dish to complement your main course. Not only do they look great, but they also make the perfect finger food. Who could resist the combination of juicy mushrooms and creamy vegan pesto on the inside? • **GLUTEN FREE** •

YIELD: 5 servings

MUSHROOMS

20 chestnut or cremini mushrooms

2 tbsp (30 ml) olive oil

1 tbsp (15 ml) balsamic vinegar

PESTO

1 cup (40 g) fresh basil leaves

½ cup (68 g) roasted pine nuts

3 tbsp (15 g) nutritional yeast

2 tbsp (30 ml) olive oil

¼ cup (60 ml) water

¼ tsp garlic powder

½ tsp salt

Dash of black pepper

TOPPING

2 tbsp (22 g) Vegan Parmesan
(page 76)

To make the mushrooms, preheat the oven to 350°F (175°C) and line a small baking sheet with parchment paper.

Remove the stems from the mushrooms. In a small bowl, combine the oil and vinegar and brush the outside of the mushrooms with the mixture. Place the mushrooms on the prepared baking sheet and roast them for 10 minutes.

In the meantime, prepare the pesto. Combine the basil leaves, pine nuts, nutritional yeast, oil, water, garlic powder, salt and black pepper in a high-speed blender and blend until the pesto is smooth. Transfer the pesto to a small jar and set aside.

Remove the baking sheet from the oven and empty the liquid from the mushrooms (get rid of as much moisture as possible). Fill each mushroom with 1 teaspoon of the pesto. Roast the stuffed mushrooms for 5 to 10 minutes. Top them with the Vegan Parmesan and serve.

BLACK BEAN HUMMUS

This hummus is an exciting twist on the classic chickpea hummus and has an earthier flavor, making it the perfect addition to any antipasto platter. • GLUTEN FREE •

YIELD: 8 servings

2 (14-oz [400-g]) cans black beans, drained and rinsed

2 cloves garlic

¼ cup (60 ml) olive oil

¼ cup (60 ml) water

¼ cup (60 ml) fresh lemon juice

2 tbsp (30 g) tahini

1 tsp ground cumin

1 tsp salt

½ tsp black pepper

Place the black beans, garlic, oil, water, lemon juice, tahini, cumin, salt and black pepper in a high-speed blender or food processor and blend until the mixture is creamy. Add more or less water, depending on the desired consistency. Transfer the hummus to an airtight jar and store it in the fridge for 3 to 4 days.

SPINACH-ARTICHOKE DIP

This is the ultimate creamy dip to pair with a few slices of fresh sourdough bread. It is incredibly rich yet not too filling and gets a nice tangy flavor from the artichoke. • GLUTEN FREE •

YIELD: 8 servings

2 cups (60 g) fresh spinach

2 cups (330 g) artichoke hearts, drained

⅔ cup (100 g) raw cashews

2 cloves garlic

2 tbsp (30 ml) olive oil

¼ cup (60 ml) water

4 tbsp (20 g) nutritional yeast

½ tsp salt

Dash of black pepper

Place the spinach, artichoke hearts, cashews, garlic, oil, water, nutritional yeast, salt and black pepper in a high-speed blender or food processor and blend until the mixture is creamy. Add more or less water, depending on the desired consistency. Transfer the dip to an airtight jar and store it in the fridge for 3 to 4 days.

QUICK TIP: The key to building a beautiful antipasto platter is to start by arranging your dips on the board. Then you can build around the dip bowls with a variety of your favorite crackers and veggies. I'd suggest using carrots, cucumbers and zucchini and slicing them into sticks lengthwise to make for easier dipping.

CHEESY LEEK-POTATO SOUP

This creamy soup is a personal favorite of mine, as I grew up eating the nonvegan version and loved it dearly. I can't believe it took me so long to create a vegan rendition, but now that I have, I can't get enough of this warming, cheesy bowl of veggie soup! It's the perfect starter on any holiday table and is extremely rich with smoky flavors. • **GLUTEN FREE** •

YIELD: 6 servings

CHEESY CREAM

1 cup (150 g) raw cashews, soaked for 6 to 8 hours (or overnight) and drained

2 cloves garlic, minced

¼ cup (20 g) nutritional yeast

1 cup (240 ml) vegetable broth

1 tsp brown miso paste

¼ cup (31 g) tapioca flour

½ tsp smoked paprika

⅛ tsp ground nutmeg

1 tsp Dijon mustard

½ tsp salt

SOUP

3 tbsp (45 ml) olive oil

1 medium onion, diced

7 oz (196 g) smoked tofu, diced

1 large leek, thinly sliced

2¼ cups (170 g) thinly sliced cremini mushrooms

3½ cups (840 ml) vegetable broth

5 small Yukon gold potatoes, peeled and diced

Salt, to taste

Black pepper, to taste

Fresh parsley, finely chopped

Fresh lemon juice

Sliced sourdough bread, for serving

To make the cheesy cream, combine the cashews, garlic, nutritional yeast, broth, miso, tapioca flour, paprika, nutmeg, mustard and salt in a high-speed blender and blend for 1 to 2 minutes, until the mixture is smooth. Set aside.

To make the soup, heat the oil in a large pot over medium heat. Add the onion and sauté until it is golden brown, 3 to 4 minutes. Add the tofu and cook for 2 minutes. Add the leek, mushrooms and a splash of the broth and cook for about 5 minutes, until the vegetables are soft. Add the potatoes and remaining broth, reduce the heat to medium-low and simmer for 20 minutes.

Pour the cheesy cream into the soup. Season with the salt and black pepper and cook for 5 minutes, stirring frequently. Garnish the soup with the parsley and lemon juice and serve with the sourdough bread.

CRANBERRY CREAM CHEESE SPREAD

Next to some uber creamy dips, an amazing vegan cheese platter has got to be my favorite appetizer! To balance out all the savory flavors that are usually found on a cheese platter, this delicious cranberry cream cheese will satisfy both your sweet and savory teeth, as it's coated in dried cranberries and thyme. • **GLUTEN FREE** •

YIELD: 10 servings

CREAM CHEESE

2 cups (300 g) raw cashews, soaked for 6 hours (or overnight) and drained (see Quick Tip)

⅓ cup (27 g) nutritional yeast

¼ cup (60 ml) fresh lemon juice

2 tbsp (30 ml) melted coconut oil

1 tbsp (17 g) white miso paste

½ tsp salt

2 cloves garlic

2 tbsp (6 g) minced fresh thyme

2 to 3 tbsp (30 to 45 ml) water, or as needed

COATING

¼ cup (30 g) raw walnuts, roughly chopped

½ cup (60 g) dried cranberries, finely chopped

2 tbsp (6 g) minced fresh thyme

To make the cream cheese, combine the cashews, nutritional yeast, lemon juice, oil, miso, salt, garlic, thyme and water in a high-speed blender. Blend until the mixture is very creamy and smooth, scraping down the sides of the blender and using the tamper tool as needed. Taste and adjust the seasonings.

Place a fine-mesh strainer over a medium bowl and line it with 2 layers of cheesecloth (or a clean, fine-textured, absorbent towel). Transfer the cream cheese mixture to the cheesecloth. Gather the corners of the cheesecloth and twist the top gently to form the cheese into a ball. Secure the cheesecloth with an elastic band. Use your hands to squeeze out any extra liquid. Place the cheeseball in the fridge for 12 hours.

Unwrap the cheeseball from the cheesecloth and place it on a piece of parchment or wax paper. Double the paper over and roll the cheese into a log (or another desired shape) and return it to the fridge for 1 to 2 hours.

To serve, unwrap the cheese log from the parchment paper. Shape it with your hands as needed.

To make the coating, combine the walnuts, cranberries and thyme on a plate and sprinkle some of the mixture on top of the cheese log. Use your hands to gently roll the log on the plate until it is coated on all sides. Place the cheese log on a serving platter with freshly cut vegetables and crackers and serve. Store leftovers, covered, in the refrigerator for up to 4 days.

QUICK TIP: Soaking nuts and seeds not only makes them easier for your blender to process (and hence achieve a smoother consistency) but also neutralizes enzyme inhibitors, releases the nuts' or seeds' nutrient potential and makes them more digestible.

CHEESY POLENTA BITES WITH GARLIC MAYONNAISE

These crispy polenta bites always seem to impress with their bright yellow hue. They are the perfect alternative to potato bites and pair beautifully with a rich and tangy garlic mayonnaise. • **GLUTEN FREE** •

YIELD: 4 to 5 servings

CHEESY POLENTA BITES

2½ cups (600 ml) vegetable broth

½ cup (120 ml) almond or soy milk

1½ cups (255 g) polenta

1 tbsp (14 g) vegan butter or 1 tbsp (15 ml) olive oil

¼ cup (20 g) nutritional yeast

¼ tsp black pepper

1 tsp garlic powder

½ tsp smoked paprika

½ tsp salt

Olive oil, as needed

GARLIC MAYONNAISE

½ cup (120 ml) sunflower oil

¼ cup (60 ml) soy milk

1 tbsp (15 ml) fresh lemon juice

Pinch of salt

½ tsp Dijon mustard

½ tsp garlic powder

½ tsp paprika

1 tsp minced fresh herbs of choice

To make the cheesy polenta bites, bring the broth and almond milk to a boil over high heat. Reduce the heat to medium and add the polenta, whisking continuously. Reduce the heat to low and cook for 5 to 6 minutes, whisking continuously, until the polenta is thick and creamy.

Take the polenta off the heat and stir in the butter, nutritional yeast, black pepper, garlic powder, smoked paprika and salt.

Line an 8 x 8–inch (20 x 20–cm) baking pan with parchment paper, letting the paper hang over the ends of the baking pan to serve as handles. Transfer the polenta to the prepared baking pan and press down evenly with a spatula. Use the parchment paper handles to press the polenta down evenly.

Refrigerate the polenta for 30 to 60 minutes. In the meantime, preheat the oven to 450°F (230°C) and grease a medium baking sheet. Lift the polenta block out of the baking pan using the parchment paper handles and place it on a cutting board. Cut the polenta into ¾-inch (19-mm)-thick strips. Transfer the strips to the prepared baking sheet and spray or brush them with the olive oil.

Bake the polenta for 15 to 20 minutes, flipping halfway through the cooking time, until it is golden brown.

In the meantime, prepare the garlic mayonnaise. Combine the sunflower oil, soy milk, lemon juice, salt, mustard, garlic powder, paprika and herbs in a narrow glass jar and blend with an immersion blender until the mayonnaise is creamy. Add more milk to make it smoother or more oil to make it firmer. Refrigerate the garlic mayonnaise until ready to serve with the polenta bites.

VEGAN EGGNOG

If there's one drink that stands out during the Christmas season, it has to be eggnog. Traditionally, eggnog is made with raw eggs, milk, cream and refined sugar, but this vegan version is a healthy, delicious alternative. • **GLUTEN FREE** •

YIELD: 3 servings

½ cup (75 g) raw cashews, soaked for 6 to 8 hours (or overnight) and drained

¾ cup (180 ml) water

½ cup (120 ml) coconut milk

3 tbsp (45 ml) pure maple syrup

½ tsp ground cinnamon

¼ tsp ground nutmeg

⅛ tsp ground cloves

2 tbsp (30 ml) bourbon (optional)

In a high-speed blender, combine the cashews, water, milk, maple syrup, cinnamon, nutmeg, cloves and bourbon (if using). Blend for 1 to 2 minutes, until the eggnog is smooth. Taste and adjust the spices and sweetness as needed. Refrigerate before serving.

CREAMY PUMPKIN LATTE

This pumpkin latte is my ultimate fall favorite! It's uber creamy, full of warming spices and almost like a sweet treat in a mug. It's not only quick to prepare but goes perfectly with a warm batch of Festive Gingerbread Cookies (page 52). • **GLUTEN FREE** •

YIELD: 2 servings

COCONUT WHIPPED CREAM

1 (14-oz [420-ml]) can full-fat coconut cream, refrigerated overnight

1 tbsp (15 ml) pure maple syrup

1 tsp pure vanilla extract

PUMPKIN LATTE

1½ cups (360 ml) almond milk

½ cup (113 g) pumpkin puree

½ tsp pumpkin pie spice

1 tbsp (15 ml) pure maple syrup

To make the coconut whipped cream, scoop only the solid portion of the chilled coconut cream into a medium bowl. Add the maple syrup and vanilla. Whip using a hand mixer until the whipped cream is light and fluffy, 1 to 2 minutes. Transfer the whipped cream to the fridge.

To make the pumpkin latte, combine the milk, pumpkin puree, pumpkin pie spice and maple syrup in a high-speed blender. Blend until the ingredients are thoroughly combined. Pour the pumpkin latte into a medium saucepan over medium heat and warm it for 2 to 3 minutes. Divide the latte between 2 mugs, add a dollop of the coconut whipped cream on top and serve.

Acknowledgments

This book was the result of an intense period of relentless cooking, taste-testing and shooting photos until late into the night. So much has gone into this project and I couldn't be prouder or happier with the outcome. I'm incredibly grateful for all the amazing people in my life that support me and have helped make this dream a reality.

Daniel, thank you for the love and constant support you give every single day! Thank you for believing in me and my strengths, even when I'm light-years away from seeing them myself. You are one of the major reasons that The Tasty K came to life in the first place, and you have been my biggest supporter since day one. Thank you for letting me take over the kitchen as my permanent studio these past months, taste-testing like a champion and putting up with my moods during stressful times.

Thank you to all of my fans and supporters around the world that have made The Tasty K into what it is today. Thank you to each of you for watching my videos, commenting on my photos, trying my recipes and sharing them with your loved ones. You mean the world to me and I couldn't wish for a more supportive or kinder community. You are my motivation and the reason I keep on sharing and creating!

Thank you to my parents and my entire family for the never-ending love and support—even when we are oceans away from one another. Thank you for being so open-minded about this new venture of mine. I know that no matter what crazy idea I'll have next, you'll be there for me. I'm truly grateful for that.

Gianna, thank you for being the best friend I could possibly hope for and being a rock when times are tough. You are an exceptional person and I'm so incredibly lucky to have you in my life!

Megan, thank you for making this book happen in the first place and always being so supportive and loving. You're such a strong role model, working incredibly hard as a new mom, foodie creator and author, and I'm grateful we connected through this platform.

Thank you, Ana Fluieras, for your guidance and help with the photo shoots! Thank you for putting up with my creative demands and being the perfect taste-tester that you are.

Finally, thank you so much to the amazingly talented, hardworking and professional team over at Page Street Publishing. Thank you for bringing this book to life, guiding me through the process in such a supportive way and working with me to create the best possible version of this book! You are rock stars, and I'll be eternally grateful for this experience and your input.

About the Author

KIRSTEN KAMINSKI is the author, recipe developer and creative mind behind The Tasty K, a social media platform for vegan cooking, sustainability and travel tips. With a background in international politics and conflict resolution, Kirsten switched careers in early 2016 to become a self-taught photographer and video editor and to show the world how easy, healthy and delicious the plant-based lifestyle can be.

Despite growing up in Germany, Kirsten has always had a passion for traveling and has lived in 8 different countries over the past 10 years. She just moved back to Germany, after many years of living abroad. Her constant travels have a great influence on her cooking and serve as never-ending inspiration for new dishes and flavors.

Having overcome health issues herself, Kirsten is trying to spread the message of how beneficial a vegan diet can be and to help people make the switch to a healthier, more sustainable and cruelty-free lifestyle. Her dynamic recipe videos and travel guides continue to go viral on social media with millions of views, and her work has been featured by *Thrive* magazine, Best of Vegan and feedfeed.

If Kirsten is not in the kitchen whipping up new recipes, you'll probably find her running outside or taking care of abandoned street animals.

You can follow Kirsten's recipes and travels on Facebook (The Tasty K) or Instagram (@thetastyk). Check out her blog, www.thetastyk.com, for more information.

Index